LS

Letters to Schnicklefritz

By Tony Woods

MARTON PUBLISHING

Copyright 2023 by Tony and Marsha Woods

This work is under copyright. No part of this publication may be reproduced, stored in a retrieval system, or transmitted in any form or by any means electronic, mechanical, photocopy, recordingor any other except for brief quotations for printed reviews, without prior permission of the publisher.

Marton Publishing ABN 28 768 241 762
martonpublishing.com

ISBN: 978-0-9944034-5-2

Requests for more information should be directed to
info@martonpublishing.com

All biblical sitations and quotes use NIV bible reference.

Specials credit to songwritter Noal Paul Stookey, Karla Thaibodeau, Kent Palmer and Denny Bouchard for lyric use of song" All My Life"

Foreword

In the motion picture GROUNDHOG DAY, the actor Bill Murray attempts to repeat a particular romantic opportunity given to him by chance. But, by merely parroting the physical process, he loses the spontaneity that had magically created it in the first place. Lesson learned. Ultimately, I think we are drawn to trust co-incidence as a positive force in our lives. Certainly, I continue to revere those happenstances that have called my heart to the 'now' of a moment.

As a song-writer – building upon stories of what is and what might be - it is then peculiarly flattering, though somewhat misleading, to be quoted and thereby mentioned as possessing a prescient wisdom. Still, I was surprised and pleased to discover a lyric from the song ALL MY LIFE appearing in these "Letters to Shickelfritz"; a reminder of the many invisible connections between hope and the reality of life.

Although I am a staunch (and often public) defender of a woman's right to independently decide matters regarding her body, I am nonetheless persuaded that a special – call it supernatural – relationship exists between mother and child, perhaps as early as the moment of conception.

I predict that the one-sided conversation you are about to 'overhear' in this book by Tony Woods will tickle your imagination, confirm your faith in co-incidence and, in speaking to a life that is yet to be realized, will encourage your trust in Love's continual presence.

Noel Paul Stookey

DEDICATION

This book is dedicated to our family. Our son Nathan, his wife, Kylie and to their children, Isaac, Ezekiel and Micah. Our daughter Nicki her husband, Chris, and son Jeremiah, the inspiration for Letters to write Schnicklefritz.

We also dedicate this book to Trevor, our first born. He didn't live long enough to have children of his own, but we rest in the assurance that he will be waiting in the Kingdom to welcome us all when we join him.

Table of Contents

Chapter One: The Great Mystery	1
Chapter Two: What's in a Name?	5
Chapter Three: The Heart of the Matter	9
Chapter Four: Work to Do	13
Chapter Five: Goodbyes and Hellos	17
Chapter Six: Sounds in the Night	21
Chapter Seven: In His Time	25
Chapter Eight: One of a Kind	27
Chapter Nine: Tin Cans and Ethernet	29
Chapter Ten: Pregnancy Brain	33
Chapter Eleven: Halfway There	37
Chapter Twelve: Thanks for the Memories	39
Chapter Thirteen: That Two-Way Street	41
Chapter Fourteen: Electric Fences	43
Chapter Fifteen: Lining the Nest	47
Chapter Sixteen: What Dreams are Made Of	49
Chapter Seventeen: Opinions and Personalities	53
Chapter Eighteen: Seeing and Perceiving	55
Chapter Nineteen: Reaching and Grasping	57
Chapter Twenty: Rocket Tests	59
Chapter Twenty-One: The Thing About Secrets	61
Chapter Twenty-Two: Knowing Voices	63
Chapter Twenty-Three: On The Wings of Eagles	67
Chapter Twenty-Four: The Village Around Us	69
Chapter Twenty-Five: Of Dogs and Dominion	71
Chapter Twenty-Six: That Wonderful Thumb	75
Chapter Twenty-Seven: Welcome to the World	79
Final Thoughts: The Greatest Question	83
Appendix	89

Table of Contents

Chapter One: The Great Mystery 1
Chapter Two: What's in a Name? 5
Chapter Three: The Blessing of the Matter 9
Chapter Four: Mom to Do 13
Chapter Five: Corn, Love, and Heifer 17
Chapter Six: Sounds in the Night 21
Chapter Seven: Telling Time 25
Chapter Eight: One of a Kind 29
Chapter Nine: The Cats and Elinore 33
Chapter Ten: Pregnancy Brain 37
Chapter Eleven: Halfway There 39
Chapter Twelve: Thanks for the Memories 43
Chapter Thirteen: The Two-Way Street 47
Chapter Fourteen: She, the Fence 49
Chapter Fifteen: Finishing the Year 51
Chapter Sixteen: What Dreams are Made Of 53
Chapter Seventeen: Opinions and Resolutions 55
Chapter Eighteen: Snow, Wind, and Searching 55
Chapter Nineteen: Repeating and Changing 57
Chapter Twenty: No Yet Easy 59
Chapter Twenty-One: The Thing About Secrets 61
Chapter Twenty-Two: Endearing Voyages 65
Chapter Twenty-Three: On The Winds of Eagles 67
Chapter Twenty-Four: The Village Around Us 71
Chapter Twenty-Five: Of Dogs and Domphuff 73
Chapter Twenty-Six: That Windmill Thumb 75
Chapter Twenty-Seven: Welcome to the World 79
Final Thoughts: The Greatest Question 83
Appendix 89

ONE
The Great Mystery

Dear Schnicklefritz,

Today, I heard of your arrival. I know of course that you've been around for a few weeks already, being carefully crafted by the Hands of the Master in that secret place the Psalmist wrote about.

Your Mom was the first to pick up on your presence, but wisely, she kept quiet for a while just to make sure. Then came the day for your first photo shoot, also known as a sonogram. According to Mom and Dad, when the machine was turned on and the signals started pinging, looking for you, they said you did a little double take, like a sideways shuffle then waited perfectly still, taking in that new experience called sound. Your ears haven't developed yet, but you could feel those vibrations, I'm sure.

I wonder what was going through your mind then? Oh, I know the doctors tell us that you wouldn't have been thinking a whole lot of anything at this stage of your development, but I'm convinced that the signal was received and acknowledged. I'll accept that the hand you raised was nothing more than random movement in the liquid world that is your home today, but I'm pretty sure when the day comes and you and I are sitting together looking at those sonograms, you'll insist that was a big high five just for me.

I remember a song by Paul Stookey of "Peter, Paul and Mary". They're really old and you probably won't know about them until you're looking in some archives somewhere when you're grown, but they were popular when I was young and the verses of the song reflect the timeless thoughts of the mother-to-be, the father, the doctor and so forth and the chorus keeps coming back to the child yet to be born, who sings,

All my life I've been living in Mystery
All my life I've been waiting for you
Soon my life will become a reality
And new...

"All my life". Yeah, Snicklefritz, you can say that, even if your life is only a few weeks old so far, and you haven't even discovered things like light and air and unfamiliar hands grabbing you and smacking your bottom. Don't worry, kid, it'll be okay. But today, your life is... a Mystery. And before you know it, it will be reality: one that your Mom and Dad and all the rest of us are working hard to make sure is a great one.

But here's the good news. Even when that mystery comes to light, and you start to discover everything life is going to send your way...even then the Mystery continues. There in the womb, you might say, and I would agree, you've never been this old before, and by God's grace, not as old as you're going to be. But the same can be said of me, your grandfather. I've never been this old before. For you and me both, the future waits out there with lots of promises. And just like you, doing that little double take when the sound waves started up, once in awhile I get signals from the One Who created me. And just like you, I do a little double take and send up the sensors. And just like you, I raise a tentative hand toward the Source.

We've got some exciting days ahead, Schnicklefritz. Let's enjoy them to the fullest, shall we? Let the Master work His magic with you, and I'll do the same.

My frame was not hidden from You when I was made in the secret place, when I was woven together in the depths of the earth. Your eyes saw my unformed body; all the days ordained for me were written in Your book before one of them came to be.

Psalms 139:15 - 16 (NIV)

TWO
What's in a Name?

Dear Schnicklefritz,

I guess we should talk about that name, seeing as how we're getting to know each other through these letters and well, I have to call you something. At this point, your grandmother and I have opted to not know whether you're a boy or a girl even though technically that's possible. Back in our day, of course, that was the way things were. Nobody knew, and it was left to the delivering doctor to announce the discovery. I'll have to admit that when your Uncle Trevor was born, I got caught up in the excitement of the moment and blurted it out before the doctor could open his mouth. He was not pleased.

This time around, though, I'm happy to wait until your Mom and Dad announce all that good stuff. Some things are worth waiting for, which is one of those great lessons you'll be struggling with soon enough. But there is one thing that can't wait, and that's the question of what I'm to call you. Without knowing your gender yet, it would be kinda hard to pick a name that would fit either possibility. And so, Schnicklefritz it is. It's not a new word, by the way; it comes all the way from the Pennsylvania Dutch folks who use it as a term of endearment when referring to children who are especially, shall we say, energetic?

It seems appropriate to put that handle on you, Schnicklefritz, at least until a more official one comes along. But you know what? I have a pretty good idea that I'll still be dusting that name off once in awhile. It was your name since before you were born, after all.

I don't know yet what your Mom and Dad are going to come up with, but I can guarantee that a lot of thought and prayer is going to go into it. That's because a person's name is one of the most important things you can carry around. In a lot of cultures, parents will wait for weeks or even months before they name their child, using that time to study and observe the baby to see if there are any unique traits that need to be documented.

Whatever name your folks come up with for you, wear it with pride, even if it's not one you might have picked for yourself. Remember that your name is going to set you apart from everyone else. It occurred to me that Adam wasn't called by name until Eve came along, but Eve was Eve from the very beginning, because she was born into a relationship. Come to think of it, that might help explain the strong silent type of persona most men try to portray, as opposed to the ladies, who are so *wonderfully* relational.

Thinking about that this morning, I started feeling sorry for you, Schnicklefritz. There you are, all alone, in a dark and silent world, and no one with whom to share this great adventure. But then I remembered, no, you're not alone at all. Your Mom has a connection (literally!) with you that no one else will ever have. Everything you need is right there at your beck and call. In fact, I hear that a baby in the womb takes whatever is necessary for proper development, and if there's anything left, it goes to Mom. That's why your mother has to take vitamins now, as much for her sake as for yours.

But there will come a day when that connection is severed, and you'll find yourself in a whole new relationship with your world and everything in it. And that's when you're going to need a name. Well, you've got one now to see you through. And I've got a way to talk to you, my precious grandchild.

Listen, Schnicklefritz, as soon as you can, I'd like you to start thinking of some names, too. "Mommy" and "Daddy" are not bad, but I expect you'll come up with some more imaginative ideas for your parents. And while you're at it, don't forget your grandfather and grandmother out here. You've got two of each, in fact, so your work is cut out for you. Whatever you come up with, remember that those names will help define the people you give them to.

We love the names we've been given already by your cousins, and you know why? Because when those names come from the lips of those kids, we know they start at the heart, carrying with them all the love a child can put into them.

So give it some thought, Schnicklefritz. No pressure.

A good name is more desirable than great riches; to be esteemed is better than silver or gold.

Proverbs 22:1 (NIV)

THREE
The Heart of the Matter

Dear Schnicklefritz,

I mentioned in the first letter our excitement at seeing the results of your first photo shoot, and how you did a little double take and raised your hand as if to say "Hi". I know of course that you're not yet ready for interaction like that. But you and I are going to have a great time talking about it one of these days, and we'll insist to everyone that it was a "Hey There!" moment for us, grandfather to grandchild.

What can't be in doubt though is the fact that everyone in that examination room heard your heartbeat loud and clear. They said you were humming along at around 140 beats per minute. That would be normal for you, and not unlike running a marathon for me. But then you are running a marathon, aren't you? So many connections to be made, so much checking and rechecking, making sure all systems are go at every stage. Let's face it, kid, you've got your work cut out for you. I guess that's why you're hard-wired to your Mom, complete with a sports package, supplying everything you need from nourishment to assembly instructions. No wonder your little heart is racing.

Here's today's "Grandpa Lesson" for you to file away until you're ready to give it some thought. In English (and English is going to be your first language, by the way; most people can never speak it fluently unless they happen to be born into it)...where was I? Oh yeah, in English, we use that word, "heart" in a lot of different ways. This week, all I can think of is that dynamo beating away inside you, driving all the parts that make you, YOU. I'd say slow it down and give it a rest, but your Maker knows what's best for you, and He's got you covered.

Besides the physical organ, though, we use the word, "heart" to describe something you're particularly good at. In a few short months, we're all going to watch you as you discover your world, and someone's going to say, "You know, Schnicklefritz has a real heart for music...or for art, or for rolling over, or for passing gas. Whatever, we'll be talking about something you're really good at.

"Heart" also comes up when we're talking about love, sometimes symbolized on things like bumper stickers with a picture of a heart. Examples include, "I (heart) chocolate", "I (heart) New Orleans", and "I (heart) you". A lot of people read things like that by saying it just like it's written, "I heart you". But most of us know and understand what the picture means, and we simply say, "I love you".

The word is way overused, as we express our love toward everything from chocolate chip cookies to relationships between boys and girls. And Schnicklefritz, it goes all the way to the top. Acts 13:22 gives us a Divine glimpse when we read that David was "a man after God's own heart".

I wanted to say that before I go on with this point: "Heart" is most often used when we're talking about our emotions. I love Hallmark movies, at least the older ones, before people started dwelling too much on political correctness. I hope you'll learn to appreciate those classics as much as I do. They're just so sappy and predictable! But they also point to a way of life that we don't see much of anymore; a time when love was pure, morality was still something to hold onto, and you didn't have to use bad language to carry on a conversation.

Here's what I'm talking about: In just about every classic Hallmark movie, a boy and a girl grow from mutual irritation to a kind of acceptance. Friendship develops into something akin to "puppy love". The couple grows closer; then at some point, they start to kiss, but every single time they get interrupted. Then finally, when they do kiss, check your watch. The movie is now about 15 seconds from the end. Predictable. Sappy. I love it.

But in the interest of full disclosure, there is one part in most Hallmark movies that, as a pastor, I have a problem with. One of the young people, usually the girl, is confused and seeks out an older, wiser person. After she expresses her struggles, the old person pats her on the arm and says, "Dear, just follow your heart."

After fifty-plus years as a pastor/counsellor, I cringe whenever I hear those words. Why, you ask? I'm glad you asked. You see, when we're talking about emotions, you need to remember that, of all the senses that we're gifted with, our emotions are the least dependable of the lot. Many unfortunates have discovered that fact when their world falls apart because they made a decision based on the emotion of the moment. I'm not saying that emotions are bad; I think in fact that having an emotional side is one thing that sets us apart from the rest of God's Creation. But don't forget that your emotions can be compared to a ten-billion-watt particle beam disintegrator. Used wisely, your emotions can take you all the way to the heart of God. Failure to keep those emotions in check never ends well.

Okay, enough of that for now. You'll have plenty of time to work on that later on. Today, just let that little heart of yours do its job, as you get ready for the Great Reveal. And let me say this without a fear or doubt: I love you.

FOUR
Work To Do

Dear Schnicklefritz,

Today I heard that you and your Mom spent the day rolling around in high places. I wonder how you reacted as the pressures dropped and rose, and once in a while you felt weightless for a few seconds, followed by a really heavy feeling.

You see, your Mom is an airline flight attendant, and today they were flying uncomfortably close to Imogene, Australia's first cyclone of the season. But that's what she does for a living. Most of the time it's a pretty cushy job with a really cool uniform made especially for you as you grow bigger every day. She's standing a lot, negotiating narrow aisles while carrying pots of hot coffee and tea. Sometimes she gets to help people who are sad or afraid. Once at least, during a particularly rough flight, she prayed with a passenger who was on the verge of a panic attack. Another time, she let a scared child who was traveling alone pull the polish off her fingernail.

She's doing what we call a 'JOB', and she loves it because she can make a difference in people's lives. But listen up Schnicklefritz, you've got a job too, and the result is going to be a lot of changed lives. We talk about "job security", and that describes your situation today. You're warm and happy, tucked up safely in the womb, where you get your meals delivered. You can sleep anytime you like and can even do cartwheels when you get bored.

God has blessed us all with work to do, and you're no exception. To some folks, it may look like you're just a passive recipient during this time of getting ready to be born. But I see it more like a partnership between you and your Mom. She's doing her best to make sure you have all you need, and if anything but *anything* threatens you, they'll have Mom to deal with.

I want you to understand this fact from the very beginning, Schnicklefritz: Even though your Mom and your Dad haven't met you face to face yet, already they are quite prepared to do whatever it takes to keep you safe. This is true because of two things: first, you've got a couple of awesome parents. Not every unborn has that assurance, and it really makes me sad to think of those others. But then I remember fact number two: God loves you, just like He loves all those other babies. His Son, Jesus, said it in a way that leaves no room for misunderstanding. He said,

"If any of you put a stumbling block before one of these little ones who believe in me, it would be better for you if a great millstone were hung around your neck, and you were thrown into the sea".

(Mark 9:42 NIV)

That verse comes as a surprise to people who don't know Jesus very well, and just think of Him as a sweet, sappy love story character. Let me say it again: God loves you. And He loves you so much that He created a built-in need in the heart of every parent to protect their young. This applies to animals too, which you'll discover some day when you wander too close to a bird's nest. The only time in Africa when we were chased by an elephant was when we mistakenly got between her and her calf. I was scared out of my wits, but your Mom was laughing the whole time.

So, break time is over. Get back to work, Schnicklefritz. And remember what I told you: God loves you so much that He gave you two fantastic parents and four awesome grandparents, along with aunts, uncles, and a whole bunch of friends and family. And in addition to that, God has given you a job to do, even there where you are today. Keep up the good work!

FIVE
Goodbyes and Hellos

Dear Schnicklefritz,

Congratulations! By now, you've completed your first trimester, and have started on the second of three. According to the experts, your face is now developing, setting up all the necessary muscles for every emotion you'll be feeling. I hadn't really thought about it until now, how expressions are so beautifully designed, working in tandem with your brain and making sure that your face is telling everyone what you want them to understand. Sometimes, your expressions speak volumes even without you knowing about it. The other day, I was sitting in an airport terminal, and a lady across from me was doing something on her computer. It was amusing; every time I looked up, she was grinning, or scowling, or even once I saw her pull out a tissue and start crying. As I got up to head for my plane, I couldn't help but glance over at her computer screen and saw that she was watching some silly movie.

Oh, Schnicklefritz, I wish I could shield you from that moment when, at least from your point of view, will be a time of absolute terror. People have tried over the years to make the birth experience less traumatic, using darkened rooms, soft music and water tanks, but since we don't hear about it very often, I guess they're finding that they just can't avoid the inevitable. So all I can say is, put your big kid britches on and come out fighting.

Actually, I believe God has engineered this whole process for our benefit. I see in the Bible that, a long time ago, the miracle of birth changed from something wonderful to something, well, less so. As God told Eve back in Genesis,

> *"To the woman He said, I will greatly increase your pangs in childbearing; in pain you shall bring forth children…"*
>
> Genesis. 3:16 (NIV)

The thing that resulted in such a change is what we call "sin", and unfortunately this is the world you're going to be born into. God still loves us, though, and I believe that's why we experience this ordeal. The more we understand what's going on, the better we can comprehend the other trauma that we all must face, which is end of life as we know it. The author of Hebrews spelled it out quite clearly.

> *"…it is appointed for mortals to die once, and after that the judgment…"*
>
> Hebrews 9:27 (NIV)

All through the Bible, I see God giving us lesson after lesson, often accompanied by some kind of illustration that helps us understand them. And that's why I think the birth process is what it is. You've got it pretty cushy, Schnicklefritz: warm and safe, with everything you need. And a few short months from now, all of that is going to come tumbling down around you, and you're going to show us the best "terror face" you can make. But even as you cry, the rest of us out here are going to be cheering you on, because we understand that this is not the end, but actually a fantastic beginning, full of love and joy and chocolate chip cookies.

Here's the other side of that God-given lesson: life goes on after birth, and when all of us move into our "appointed time" to die, I believe most of us are going to face that time with bewilderment, terror and even anger. But over there on the other side, the heavens are going to be cheering us on, knowing that death, for the child of God, is not the end, but the beginning of everything good.

So I guess I have to say it, and I'll repeat it one of these days when we sit together over a stout mug of hot chocolate. Thank you, Schnicklefritz. Thank you for giving us this priceless lesson. As those face muscles are developing this week, work on that "terror face". But while you're at it, start exercising those other expressions, like surprise, joy and love. You'll need them all.

And then just for grins, show me your best "crazy face".

SIX
Sounds in the Night

Dear Schnicklefritz,

Well, I think you're going into week number fifteen, and if that's the case, then your ears are coming online. I'm told that the main thing you'll be able to hear now will be your Mom's heartbeat. Let that be a comfort to you kid, knowing that she's right there for you, 24/7. When her pulse picks up, yours does too. And when she's calm or sleeping, you'll detect that as well.

With this new thing called "sound", we, your family, are going to be doing some experiments. Music is a great way to start, so I'm going to be suggesting we dust off some old Peter, Paul and Mary albums, or maybe Simon and Garfunkel. Those folks knew how to write good music back in the sixties, and it's only fair that you should hear their stuff, right?

I'm finding it interesting that one of our first "discussions" concerning you involves what you hear, and how much we will be able to protect you. I don't think anyone has seriously suggested cranking up some heavy metal concerts and holding it next to you. I mean, that stuff drives me crazy! Classical music is a big contender, on the assumption that it will communicate peace and calm. But I like what your Mom and Dad decided on, that they would put together some well-known Christian tunes for your enjoyment. That's a great idea, and what harm could it do? After all, you're never too young to start hearing the kind of music that has permeated our lives, and hopefully, will be a big part of your life as well.

There's a saying going around that you'll come across at some point, and it's this: "God gave us two eyes and two ears, but only one mouth". The truth of that saying is never more obvious than when we look at you, Schnicklefritz. There you are, cozily tucked away and waiting for the Big Day. Eyes wouldn't do you much good right now, and so God has wisely left your eyelids sealed shut until just before the time you'll need them. The same goes for your mouth. That irreducibly complex system involving lungs, vocal cords and a way to convert sounds into words is not going to manifest itself until you're in a position to express yourself.

What you need right now is set of ears. There's lots going on within earshot all around you, and this week you've been given the gift of hearing those things. The first thing you heard, as I mentioned, was your Mom's heartbeat, bringing with it a sense of peace and security. It's funny, but I just now remembered something from my childhood. We'd gotten a brand new puppy, and he spent a lot of time whining and yelping. But at the advice of a friend, we put a clock in his bed, and the change was amazing! No, it wasn't because he could now see what time it was, silly! The clock we placed beside him was an old windup variety that made a rather loud ticking noise. When that puppy heard the "tick tock tick tock", it must have reminded him of his mother's heartbeat and he was immediately comforted.

Come to think of it, for a number of reasons, we had to take that puppy home when he was just a newborn. His eyes hadn't opened yet, an event that usually happens at about two weeks. Just wait, as soon as you are born, someone (probably me, if no one else says it) will comment, "What a perfect child, and his eyes are already open!"

So today I'm saying a special prayer for you, Schnicklefritz. May everything you hear today bring you peace and joy. Whether it's some great sixties music, or the sounds of your

Mom and Dad speaking words of love, please listen carefully. The Bible has a lot of references about what we say and do, but what you read most are passages that encourage us to listen. Listen to what God says. Listen with your heart and take everything onboard.

And anytime you want to hear some great sixties music, just give Mom a swift kick.

SEVEN
In His Time

Dear Schnicklefritz,

In my last letter, I commented on the fact that your ears are coming online, and that the first sound you heard was your Mom's heartbeat. That just makes my own heart beat a little faster, to think that the two of you now have an audio connection. You'll be hearing a lot from now on, Schnicklefritz, from words of love directed right at you, to a lot of conversations that may or may not be about you at all, to all manner of music, some of it for your benefit and a lot of it just background noise. I know you'll be taking it all in, though, filing it away for future reference.

This week, according to what I'm reading, your eyes are now fully developed, and starting to track. Side to side at first, then up and down. But once again, by God's grace, you're not seeing anything yet, since your eyelids form a watertight seal, keeping any unnecessary debris out.

I once read that the leaves of trees that grow in the cold regions have an amazing system for protecting their branches from the heavy snows of winter. Between the leaf and the tree branch, there is a line of what they call "abscission" cells. And just like scissors, when the season starts to change, those cells are activated and a neat line is cut, allowing the leaf to drop to the ground.

Schnicklefritz, you've got a set of abscission cells of your own, right along your eyelids. When the time is right, those cells are going to activate and voila! You'll be able to open your eyes and get ready to take in the sights. And what sights wait for you, Kid! I can't wait to start showing you the world God made just for us.

But it has to come at the right time, in the right order. Just like those peepers of yours are kept covered until about the seventh month, leaving you plenty of time to learn how to give me a wink before you make the scene, everything else in life has a proper order about it.

God made us with the capacity to take things in as we're able to. Jesus even told His disciples in John 16:12, "I have many things to say to you, but you cannot bear them now." I'm not Jesus, but I too have many things to share with you, Schnicklefritz. And you'll have to be patient with me when I start getting ahead of myself, going on and on about things like fuel injection engines, and abscission cells and the need for proper Greek verb declination in the Gospels, when what I should be doing is pushing a Hot Wheels car back and forth with you, picking flowers for your Mom and singing "Jesus loves me this I know for the Bible tells me so."

Just like the old hymn goes, "God makes all things beautiful in His time", the same is true for you and me, Kid. There's a world of things out there that's going to blow your socks off, and when the time is right, you'll see them and hear them and touch them. And the same is true for me. The same God Who is knitting you together right now is working on me, one step at a time. He's counting the days when He'll be able to say to me, "Hey, you wanta see something really cool?"

Keep exercising those eyeballs, Schnicklefritz: side to side, up and down. Because one of these days, a light show is going to be coming at you from all sides. I can hardly wait. Until then, keep up the good work!

EIGHT
One of a Kind

Dear Schnicklefritz,

Remember I said a couple of letters ago that you weren't a passive participant in this whole birth thing? I encouraged you to keep up the good work and stay to the plan. From what I'm hearing, you must have taken that on board! That rubbery cartilage that's going to be your structural re-bar is turning to stone, and it's getting covered quick time with muscles and tendons. Keeping in mind the extra workload, I hear that your umbilical cord is now thicker and stronger in order to keep up with the increasing demand for supplies and sustenance.

And those little kicks you've been experimenting with the last couple of weeks are now becoming the stuff of an NFL place kicker. Mom says that not only can you kick in all the right spots, but now you've got some serious power behind them. I know she says she loves it when you really connect, but go easy on her, Kid; she's got a lot of work to do too.

I notice also that, about now, the skin on your fingers is developing into lines and forming unique patterns. Later on, those lines will be a way of identifying you as "Schnicklefritz: the One and Only." When you're born, the nurses will dip your feet in ink and mark your birth certificate with them. Later on, though, fingerprints will be the primary method for identification, since nobody else in the whole world has an identical set.

Isn't that cool? Step by step, God is knitting you together, and as He works, He puts His stamp on you, saying to everyone, "This child is mine. Mom and Dad have the responsibility for taking care of you and raising you up in the way you should go, but never forget that I am the Creator."

I know some people rebel against that idea, insisting that they are "self-made" and not subject to anyone else, even God. But listen, Schnicklefritz, I've known people who try to live their own lives, pretending to be free from all authority, but trust me: it never ends well.

For me, I find it very encouraging to know that you and I have a Creator Who put His stamp on us, and parents who follow His guidance in raising us to be all we can be. By God's grace, I am a one-of-a-kind creation. You can call me whatever you like, but I will always carry the Master Craftsman's mark, starting with the fingerprints and going all the way down to an atomic level. Schnicklefritz, there's never been another like you, and there will never be another again, ever.

The God who "determines the number of the stars; and calls each of them by name" (Psalms 147:4) is the same God who even now is "forming your inward parts; knitting you together in your mother's womb" (Psalms 139:13).

I'm just as proud as punch when I hear of your progress, Kid. And I thank God every day that He's right there with you, every step of the way. And I believe that you and God have a very special relationship that none of us on this side knows about. You know better than me what it's like to be clay in the Potter's Hands. After you're born, you'll be like those children that Jesus says we need to become like if we're going to see Heaven. Don't lose that connection, Schnicklefritz. One of these days, you'll have a unique opportunity to teach me some good stuff that only you can. I can't wait to hear it!

NINE
Tin Cans and Ethernet

Dear Schnicklefritz,

I just upgraded my house's internet from cable to fibre optic, and Wow! What a difference! Before, my computer was hooked up to the same cable that made the tv work. It really was impressive, when you think about it, and especially when you consider that I used to use two tin cans connected by a string when I was a little boy and actually I was quite proud of that system.

Finally, though, this thing called a "fibre optic cable" has made its way into the house. Now, when I fire up the computer, it starts communicating with something out there called the "Ethernet", using particles of light called "photons".

"Standby the photon torpedoes, Scotty! Lock and load!" Never mind all that, Schnicklefritz; I'll save some old Star Trek re-runs for you when you get here. You'll love em.

But where was I? Oh yeah, from what I'm hearing, you're involved in some circuitry setups that'll make my fibre optics look like tin cans and string. It all started with something called "myelin", a mixture of fat and protein that provides insulation and protection for your developing nervous system.

"See, Mom? I told you that fat was a good thing!" But back to where was I...

What you're putting the finishing touches on this week is a smokin' hot freeway that reaches from your brain to your spinal cord, and from there to all your extremities. What you've had until now has been a basic setup that allowed a nice, (comparatively) slow cable for bringing in building materials, setting parameters and making sure your body has what it needs for the next phase of development.

That next phase is going to be run from a hardened bunker (think: brain), and it's going to organize itself into three main functions, sensory input, information processing and motor functions. The sensory department is there to help guard you from things like hot stoves. Oh, Schnicklefritz, I wish I could protect you from that first contact with a hot stove, but as near as I can tell, every one of us has had that experience. And you know what? The next time you come near something hot, that sensory department is going to start yelling, "Back off! It's hot!"

The information processing department is gearing up to take on board every bit of stuff you see and hear, then decide whether it needs to be kicked upstairs or filled away for future reference. I'm told that nothing you see or hear will ever be erased; just placed farther back into the archives. Maybe that's why I can still remember the words to a toothpaste jingle I heard 60 years ago...even though I sometimes can't remember why I came into the kitchen.

The motor functions department of your neuro system is going to control all those things that are really important but that you don't need to bother yourself about, like heartbeat and breathing. It will also tell you just how much pressure to give your fingers in order to pick up a baby bird without hurting it. And by the way, I'll be using my own system when I first lift you into my arms for a big hug.

I could go on and on, just trying to describe the amazing technology that's making you who you are, and what you're going to become, but then I'd miss the most important part, which is why it's all there in the first place. God is a Master Craftsman, and YOU are His finest accomplishment. Never forget the fact that "God don't make no junk". I say that because there may come a time in your life when you feel, well, less than perfect. And you may be tempted to cry out to Him, "Why did you make me like this?"

If you ever start feeling that way in the years to come, pull out these letters and remind yourself of everything that's come together. The technology itself is pretty awesome, for sure, but the Biggest and Best can't be graphed out on a schematic. I thank God today, Schnicklefritz, for the miracle that's you, and can't wait to meet you in person. Until then, "Load the photon torpedoes, Scotty!"

TEN
Pregnancy Brain

Dear Schnicklefritz,

Well, there's been a lot of talk the last few weeks about You and what's going on with that mighty, mysterious, magnificent body of yours. I think now I need to give your Mom equal time.

I say this because I've been reading a lot lately about "Pregnancy Brain". It seems that around this time in the process, Mothers-to-Be (including your Mom) are beginning to experience things like lost keys, forgotten appointments and misplaced wallets. They insist that they weren't this way before, and so there's a distinct tendency to place the blame on you.

Yeah, I know, you were at the library and so couldn't possibly have anything to do with Mom's Madness. My own response is to say, "Hey, wait til you've been around 70 years or so. Now THAT'S a condition that ...that...well, I forgot what I was going to say.

But in all fairness, there is quite a bit of evidence to suggest that Pregnancy Brain is real. It is a known fact, for example, that brain scans taken of women can show if they have given birth to babies or not. It's not a bad thing, mind you, just a slight shrinking of Mom's brain in certain areas of cognitive thinking. Some have even said that it's a good and natural thing, because it results in an increased specialization of tasks related to child-rearing. Wouldn't that be interesting if God is saying, "Okay Mom, it's time to focus. Let's straighten things up a bit"?

All scientific studies aside, I can't help but think that what we're seeing here is simply the result of Mom being blown away by what's happening. At the very least, your Mom is dealing with a whole new set of experiences, physical and emotional, that's sure to put her life in perspective.

Think back to the Apostle John, when he was told by Jesus to "Watch carefully, and write this down" (Revelation 1:11). He's just seen an angel with a voice like a trumpet, and is being shown Jesus with, "a long robe and with a golden sash across his chest. His head and his hair white as white wool, white as snow; his eyes like a flame of fire, his feet like burnished bronze, refined as in a furnace, and his voice like the sound of many waters. In his right hand he's holding seven stars, and from his mouth comes a sharp, two-edged sword, and his face is like the sun shining with full force."

Now give John's shirt a tug and ask him, "Hey! What time are Peter and his folks coming over for dinner?" Pregnancy Brain ... yeah, right.

The fact of the matter, Schnicklefritz, is that your Mom is going through something she's never been through before. It's amazing. It's almost unbelievable. And it's a little scary. I think we can cut her some slack if she misplaces her phone today. As for you, this is just business as usual. Every day, week by week, you're being knit together in that secret place where only God can see completely. He's got you well in Hand, and He won't let you get too upset over the day-to-day adventure. Mom, on the other hand, is dealing with things like weight gain, nursery planning, unexpected kicks, running scenario after scenario with every plot imaginable. Then when she stops for a minute to think about it, her mind is overwhelmed by the fresh realization that she's carrying a brand new life around. And believe me: if it came to it, even now, she would gladly lay her life down to protect you.

So before you go to sleep, as much as you're able, think about the impact you're already having on Mom, and Dad, and Grandparents. It's a powerful force, Schnicklefritz, and one that only grows with time. Even now, I have to stop a second and say, "Whoa! Cool!"

ELEVEN
Halfway There

Dear Schnicklefritz,

By my calculations, you've just passed 20 weeks, which means (wait a minute...carry the eight...add two...yeah) you're over halfway there! If anyone ever sat in a bathtub for 20 weeks, they would realize that your skin might be getting a little pruney by now. And indeed it would, except for a brand new coat of vernix caseosa, which is like the best varnish ever made and which is going to protect that beautiful skin of yours. Too bad we won't get to see it (unless of course you decide to come early), since most of it will magically disappear just before you're born.

That's just one more example of how your body is gearing up for the Big Day. By now you have fully functional ears (though there's not too much to hear just yet), eyes that are already tracking, resting behind a watertight case until just before you need them, and as of last week, a super highway nervous system connecting every circuit you'll be needing. AND around this week, your lungs are getting ready to take on this stuff we call "air". Those little hummers are going to come in real handy when you feel the need for a good cry, or a good laugh, or, before you know it, the need to coordinate those lungs with your voice box, lips and tongue to start sounding out words.

Now listen carefully, Schnicklefritz... GGGRRAAND... PAAA! Just kidding. No I'm not.

I want to thank you again, Kid, for the reminders you continue to dish out to this old man. I've been a Christian for lots of years now, and I feel pretty comfortable with the way God has made the world. Yeah, we've made a mess of things, but He still loves us and is promising a jaw-dropping future. In the meantime, I just have to look around to see His handiwork and think to myself. I'm thinking, if what I can SEE is any evidence of what God is like, how much more is there out there that I can't see yet?

And then I look at you, Schnicklefritz (or at least what I imagine you look like today), and I can just hear God saying with a chuckle, "You ain't seen NOTHIN yet!" I mean, how could anyone in their right mind follow your progress and think it all came about by accident? Eyes and lungs, for example...put together perfectly in just the right order, in total darkness and without a single breath full of air. And then, just before you need them, something clicks, and you'll hear, "Fasten your seatbelt, Kid; here we go!"

Well, my seatbelt's already fastened, and my breath is bated in anticipation. The book says you can do it now, so give it a try: one little somersault for Mom.

TWELVE
Thanks for the Memories

Dear Schnicklefritz,

I asked your Mom today what new and exciting things she was learning about you, and her answer surprised me. Here's what she said:

"Now that all the major systems are up and running, Schnicklefritz is starting to build memories."

What? How can a kid still in the womb have anything to remember? Quite a lot, as it turns out. By now, your eyes are tracking all over the place, your ears are tuning into every sound that comes your way, and that Super Highway nervous system of yours is just begging to kick in. Although we haven't seen it yet ourselves, kids at your state of development have been observed putting their hands over their ears when around unpleasant noises. That's why, of course, I've insisted that there be no heavy metal rock concerts in your vicinity!

All those stimuli are being taken on board, filed into the appropriate boxes, and recalled when necessary. That's memory at work, Kid. Already, we can see that the sound of Mom's voice produces what can only be described as a sense of peace in your activities. The same goes for Dad. And although I haven't had much "face time" with you, there does seem to be a reaction to the sound of my voice... something like, "Wait a minute...is that who I think it is?"

God knew what He was doing when He built us with memory banks. At least 169 times in the Bible we're told to "remember". Some of the memories are good, and some

...well not so much. But they all come together to help teach us right from wrong, and to either foster or avoid certain situations, especially when they're associated with something you've experienced.

Put enough memories together, and you've got what I call "history". Your Grandmother and I have clocked up about 55 years of it so far, and it just gets more precious every day. But the thing that I find really cool is that all that history-making memory started way back when I was your age, Schnicklefritz. One experience built on another, built on another, nothing ever forgotten, but filed away in appropriate boxes.

It's all there for our comfort, our enjoyment, or as the case may be, for our discipline. As a five-year-old, I could remember clearly the fact that, when Mom's voice rose an octave, it was time to listen up. To fail to do so often had unpleasant consequences.

You and I, Kid, are building memories, and like the Psalmist who wrote,

"On my bed [or your case, in the womb] I remember you; I think of you through the watches of the night."

Psalm 63:6(NIV)

I believe those of us out here don't give you enough credit for lying around and remembering. But research is showing us that you're pretty good at it already. Today, Schnicklefritz, may your memories be sweet, or at least instructive.

THIRTEEN
That Two-Way Street

Dear Schnicklefritz,

Well, I hope you're proud of yourself, Kid. You gave us a real scare the other day! It occurred to your Mom that she hadn't felt you move in over 24 hours. She called up the doctor and was told to come on in where they would run some tests.

After a few foetal monitors and an ultrasound, you were located and tracked, hiding! The technicians in the imaging department swore they saw a smirk on your face and read "Gotcha!" on your lips.

Okay, maybe I'm over-reacting, but it does bring up a point I was about to make. Schnicklefritz, the more "connected" you're getting with us, the more we long for the day when we can hold you in our arms and teach you to say "Grandpa". That last part may have been a personal observation, but the fact remains: communication is becoming more and more a two-way street. And what is true in relationships out here is also true from where you sit (or "float", as it may be).

When God created us, He created us for fellowship. "It's not good for the man to be alone", He said in Genesis 2:18. Then He got to work making Eve. And take note: the "man" didn't even have a name until Eve came along. Without each other, we wouldn't need our names, which is why I'm calling you "Schnicklefritz" until your Mom and Dad come up with something better. I'd like to think that you and I already have a special connection, and I plan to build on that after you're born.

A big part of relationship-building is communicating, and so far, you've done a great job, using whatever you have on hand (including the hand itself, which I'm sure you're using to wave at us). As I said last week, your memory base is already set up and you're adding to that daily those experiences and sensations that you'll call on in order to draw conclusions about stuff.

A lot of us out here seem to forget the importance of keeping those lines of communication open, and what results is a lot of misunderstanding. When I moved to a new church a few years back, a man there told me, "You know, we never asked for you to come here." I was crushed, but rather than talk about it with him, I harboured all kinds of feelings about him that he never deserved. Years later, as we were about to transfer to another ministry point, I heard him speak up in a meeting and finish his sentence: "You know, we never asked for you to come here, but what an amazing God, Who knew what we needed even before we knew it. He sent you, and what a blessing you've been!"

How do you think I felt? No, even worse than that.

Now let me finish my sentence to you, Kid. I'm not accusing you of playing "Elmer Fudd" with us and staying "veeahwee quiet" just to have some fun at our expense. I think that part of your development will come later, after you've had a chance to see what you've got to work with. I've got some great tricks to teach you; remind me later.

But what I *am* saying is that we love you so much already, we can't let a day go by without hearing from you. Even a swift kick to Mom when she least expects it is better than staying silent. Don't tell her I said so...just give her a swift kick.

FOURTEEN
Electric Fences

Dear Schnicklefritz,

Well, last time, I told you how important it is that we keep up communications. You must have listened to me! The experts tell me that this is the week your brain wave activity is coming online, which means that not only can you sense everything around you, but it's also now possible to respond. Granted, your responses may not be all that complicated, but they can be effective. Giving Mom a good swift kick in answer to a loud noise is about as developed as it comes, but she gets the message!

Now that your eyes are open and functioning (complete with eyelashes this week!), a good strong light pointed in your direction never fails to get a rise, along with a heartfelt, "Hey! Shut that thing off!" …. if only you could.

Your living space is becoming a little cramped, and I hate to say it, Kid, but it's only going to get worse over the next few weeks. On the other hand, while you may find somersaulting a bit more challenging, Mom's tummy is now in just the right position for "peddling", using her like a treadmill. The doctors say this is a good thing, though, since you're building those walking muscles. So crank it up and feel the burn!

And speaking of "the burn", I need to point out, Schnicklefritz, that your life is already experiencing some things that may not be all that pleasant. Cramped living conditions are a constant reminder that there are limits to everything. As you get older, you'll probably start testing those limits in an attempt to establish yourself. This is natural, and all of us out here will do our best to make sure you don't hurt yourself when you come up against some barbed wire. For sure, it's gonna be painful for us to see you trying your best to break out of the space we know is best for you. But we'll be firm, because we know there's a world of hurt on the other side of those barriers.

Poor Saul (later to become the Apostle Paul) had to get the message straight from God. Struck down while on his way to make a bad day for some Christians, he lay there on the road, blind and terrified, when he heard his Heavenly Father say to him gently,

"Saul, Saul, why are you persecuting me? It hurts you to kick against the goads"

Acts 26:14 (NIV).

Good lesson for Saul; good lesson for all of us, and that includes you, dear Schnicklefritz. Those "goads" we read about are like sharp sticks that never bother us, unless of course we kick against them. Growing up on a small Texas farm, I had a calf: nicest little white-faced Hereford that ever graced my pasture. And it was a great paddock (as we say here in Australia), carefully seeded with clover and alfalfa and plenty of water and a salt block nearby. But, as you might expect, that calf was determined to get to the other side of the fence to what appeared to him to be greener grass.

I wished I could speak Hereford, so I could explain to him that the pasture he was eyeing was not mine, and in fact was not as good as the one he was in. But we couldn't seem to communicate until I set up an electric fence. The first time he discovered it was as he was stretching out to the wire with a cold, wet nose. The second time was just to make sure that wire really bit, and the third and fourth times were simple rebellion at work. He finally learned his lesson, and I could turn the power off, knowing he would never venture near that wire again.

Schnicklefritz, there are going to be some electric fences in your life, and I hurt for you already, knowing that you're just going to have to stretch your nose out until you get bit. But please remember, whether it's greener pastures, hot stoves, busy streets or Heaven itself, the barriers you find are put there for your protection and maintained by folks who love you so deeply they'll lay down their lives to make sure you enjoy only what you've been given.

Those "folks" include your Mom and Dad, grandparents, and even Jesus. So have a ball today, Kid. Don't sweat the cramped quarters and look forward to the day when a whole new world opens up to you.

FIFTEEN
Lining the Nest

Dear Schnicklefritz,

Today it's me writing. I'm your Grandma and I've been here the whole time, just waiting for a chance to talk to you.

You see, little Schnicklefritz, I wanted to add my letter to the ones your Grandfather has already written to you. What you need to know today is that I love you at least as much as anyone else in the room, and I talk to you in my head all the time.

In fact, I think of you especially every morning when we open our bathroom window to let in some air. Right outside the window, there's a thick patch of bamboo, and a few weeks ago, we spotted a dove working her way inside it, carrying a beak full of twigs. Sure enough, she was building a nest, and now is sitting on a clutch of eggs!

We can't see the nest, exactly, because she picked just the right spot that was out of sight from every angle. It's already weathered some pretty severe rainstorms, so we know she's done a good job of providing for her young. Most Moms are like that, you know.

But what has become part of our daily ritual every morning is listening to her happy cooing. It seems that both the Mom Dove and Dad Dove coo a lot; people say it seems to be some sort of bragging rights that they're sitting on eggs (Sounds like your folks, when I think about it).

But I especially like listening to Mother Dove talking to her babies every day, even though they haven't hatched yet, just like your Mom is doing now. I checked her out in our bird book and found that doves mate for life, and are especially known for being great mothers. Sounds like your own Mom, Kid, although I don't think your Mom is eating 20% of her body weight every day just to make up some good nutrition to feed you when you hatch. But I did read that of all the nutritious food she eats, the best of everything goes first and directly to you. Then if there's anything left over, Mom gets it. That's why a lot of mothers develop problems with their teeth during pregnancy, since they're not getting enough calcium. Don't worry about it, though; she's taking plenty of vitamins, so she'll be okay.

It's autumn here, and I thought that was a bit odd for picking this time to have babies, since winter is coming on. But wait, you'll be arriving mid-winter as well. I guess doves and Moms all over know that your comfort is assured, no matter the weather. With great parents to cuddle and swaddle you and coo to you when the cold wind blows, you've got it made!

Come to think of it, maybe I'll go out now and do a little shopping for some new 'twigs' to line your nest!

SIXTEEN
What Dreams Are Made Of

Dear Schnicklefritz,

I hope you enjoyed last week's letter from Grandma. I'm back this time, and still just blown away by the progress you're making, week by week. I'm told that by now, your brain makes up 28% of your total body weight. A good thing too, since by now you're packing in around 100 billion brain cells, and they're all coming online!

New abilities this week include blinking, coughing, sucking, hiccupping and breathing. Yeah, I know breathing may not seem all that significant, especially when you haven't tasted real air yet. And that stuff you're floating in and breathing into your system is getting less and less pure grade. I hesitate to mention that, well, Kid, it's not your fault that there's no ensuite toilet provided where you are. Just saying...

But the other HUGE event these days is that you're starting to dream! How do we know that? As I said before, you're developing fairly predictable sleep cycles, and your brain wave activity can now confirm that. Furthermore, now that your eyes are fully functional, it has been observed in other babies in your stage of development that while you're asleep, observers can see rapid eye movement behind those beautiful eyelashes of yours.

The same thing can be seen in everyone else, from kids to adults, and in every case, it's an indicator that dreams are happening. Your Dad expressed the question that was on all of our minds: "What would he be dreaming about?"

Good question. What kind of dream could a baby put together, based on life in a closed, dark and airless system? I guess you could dream about the sensory perceptions that are becoming more and more a part of your daily routines. But I have another idea, totally un-provable but quite logical, when you think about it. Schnicklefritz, I think you're having some one-on-one with your Creator, and I'm not talking about Mom and Dad.

Consider this: Jesus held children up to be the epitome of the Kingdom of God. He said,

"unless WE become like CHILDREN, we'll never set foot into Heaven"

Matthew 18:3-4(NIV).

And then think about all the folks in the Bible who were given direct messages from God through dreams. Just thumbing through my Bible, I came across at least fifteen examples, and then saw where God tells it straight:

"Hear my words: When there are prophets among you, I the LORD make myself known to them in visions; I speak to them in dreams"

Numbers 12:6 (NIV).

So there's no doubt that dreams are often a conduit to God, and that children are among His favourites. I could also point to the fact that children have no problem accepting the existence of God, but then as they get older, they tend to "forget". It makes me sad when parents tell me, "We're going to wait until our child grows up to tell him about God. He can make up his own mind then." That's like saying, "We're not going to feed her until she's an adult. She can decide then if she wants to eat."

Oh, Schnicklefritz, I wish I could tap into your mind right now! What words of wisdom are you taking on board? How are those 100 billion brain cells being used while you sleep? I know you probably won't be able to tell me in words I can understand, but listen: after you're born, I'm going to be watching and listening to everything I can. Who knows? Maybe God has a message for me to be delivered by you!

Sweet dreams kid.

SEVENTEEN
Opinions and Personalities

Dear Schnicklefritz,

There's a scene from a movie that has stayed deep in the hearts of folks all over. The movie was "Rocky" and it's about the comeback of a down and out boxer by the name of Rocky Balboa, played by Sylvester Stallone. One morning, he makes the decision to get back to fighting trim. The room is dark when his alarm goes off. He staggers over to the fridge and starts cracking raw eggs into a glass, drinking it down to the horrified gasps of movie watchers.

Then he hits the road, jogging slowly at first to the music, "Runnin's hard now ... runnin's hard now". By the time the song is over, he's climbing the 72 stone steps leading to the Philadelphia Museum of Art, followed by a crowd of kids inspired by his efforts.

The inspiration lives on. Today there's a statue of Sly in front of the museum and the "Rocky Steps" as they've come to be known.

I bring this up, Kid, because lately whenever I think of you, that song starts running through my head and brass chords keep repeating, "Dah da DAH dah". As I check to see what progress you're making this week, I see Rocky Balboa. Your skin, wrinkled at first, is now smoothing up, pushed out by some pretty awesome muscles, fastened to some rock-hard bones.

Your exercise regimen is picking up as well. No longer are you content with somersaults and "treadmilling" along your Mom's womb; now you're doing some serious crunches, handstands and a few karate kicks that would make Bruce Lee envious.

And I think it's no coincidence that, along with the new look, there's a new thought process becoming evident among those 100 billion activated brain cells of yours. Some would call it..."personality". Something like that is hard to identify at this stage, but there's plenty of evidence that you're beginning to express an opinion. Loud noises, bright lights, even spicy lasagne is resulting in a predictable pattern in the way you react. About all you have to work with so far is "body language", but you're using it to the fullest.

As parents, we've often remarked that our kids, while hopefully modelling the lifestyles and values we try to place in them, nevertheless are possessed with personalities that are all their own. I can see it very clearly in my own children, and grandchildren, and I have no doubt that you will be YOU and no one else. And that process, I believe, has already started in you, Schnicklefritz. It's something that none of us out here have any control over. You are being knitted together in God's image with a unique personality that will help define what you're going to be.

But I take comfort in the fact that, even though there are an infinite number of personalities out there, the thing that seems to keep people on an even keel, for the most part, is a sense of purpose and an assurance of being loved. God has given you the first part already, stated so wonderfully in Ephesians 2:10. And He is allowing us to participate in the second part by loving you every day of your life, through whatever comes your way.

And if you don't believe me now, just wait; you got a lot of cuddles coming your way!

EIGHTEEN
Seeing and Perceiving

Dear Schnicklefritz,

Hi! It's Grandma again. We had such a lovely talk the other day, I convinced Grandpa to let me tell you about seeing you on the big screen! A few days ago, several of us went to see a 3D ultrasound of you.

I didn't know about this custom because it's such a new thing. Even your cousins never made such an appearance before they were born. Nowadays, it seems to be the social event of the season, at least for the half dozen lucky observers who are invited. It was a real "party atmosphere", we laughed that all that was lacking was a plate of nibblies and maybe some "champas" as they say here in Australia.

We settled around a giant screen, four of us: two grandmas (one of whom is about to be a grandma for the first time), an auntie and of course your dad. Your Mom popped up on the examining table and we began the search for...YOU.

For the first several minutes, I felt like I was lying on a blanket in a meadow, trying to find the horse or the football in the clouds. Because I've never done this, I had no idea what I was looking for, but then, as the technician moved the wand around, an ear went flying by. I blinked and there you were!

But alas, you had decided to sleep at this particular moment and there was nothing your Mom or the attendant could do in the next half hour to make you come to the party. You were very adorably curled up with your face to your Mommy's back, left hand crossing under your chin and covering your right ear, along with your right hand AND a foot comfortably placed right in front of your face. It looks like you're going to be like your Daddy, maybe a bit shy!

Thank you for letting us have this 'visit' with you, even if you slept through it. I couldn't help but mention the irony of how much we're going to adore this sleeping form when you're out in the world, and how we'll be hovering again, but this time whispering "Shhhhhh, be quiet; the Baby's sleeping!"

The Bible doesn't have a lot to say about 3D imaging since, of course it hadn't been invented yet. But I can see it everywhere I look in His Word and see there the difference between our view of things and God's view. I think we see the world like those Egyptian hieroglyphics, flat against the wall, heads turned to the side and arms plastered left and right. And so I have to conclude that it's not just in the way we SEE things, but in the way we perceive them.

"...for the LORD does not see as mortals see; they look on the outward appearance, but the LORD looks on the heart"
Samuel 16:7 (NIV).

It's so sad to me that a lot of folks can't see you the way I do, Schnicklefritz. As we've been writing these letters to you each week, studying up to see the miracle that is you taking shape right before our eyes, we're starting to see beyond the flat, one-dimensional view and coming face to face with a real 3D image from Heaven. So get your foot out of your face and get ready to give Mae a big cuddle!

NINETEEN
Reaching and Grasping

Dear Schnicklefritz,

Well, according to the latest medical observations, you've "gone vertical", another way of saying you're head down, buckled in and ready to ride. Of course, that doesn't mean your birth is imminent, but that it could come any time between today and a couple of months from now. That fine hair (called "lanago") covering your body is clearing out in favour of new growth around the top of your head. Don't worry; we'll have a barber standing by.

In the meantime, all systems are go, and you're spending your days packing on the weight (around ½ pound a week, by the last count). It's getting pretty cramped in there, and as a result, your exercise routines are slowing down a bit. Activity is being measured in "kick counts": now hovering at around five per hour. This is also an indicator that your rest cycles are becoming more and more predictable, and in fact will carry on even after you're born. Mom is trying to keep up her own exercise program, but it's getting tougher the more you're growing.

One new development seems to be the discovery of your hands. Until now, you've used them mostly for waving to Grandpa, shielding your eyes and ears from the sound and light show going on all around you these days, and sucking your thumb.

Lately, though, you've learned to grasp things, and one of the first things to drift by were your feet. I predict one day you'll be pulling a big toe up to your face and giving it a big bite. Thus will follow the next major discovery, that of pain.

But for me, the most exciting thing about your hands is the way you're learning to use them to communicate with the outside world. Whenever Dad pokes on Mom's tummy, you've been known to poke back, at the same spot where the offending poke occurred. You may see this as simply guarding your perimeter, but listen up Kid; this is the way we play. You're going to have to put up with a lot in the months to come. Everyone who drops in to see you is just going to have do something to try and get a rise. People will be making faces at you, trying to scare you with sudden "boo!"s and yes, poking you all over.

And invariably, they will offer a finger for you to grasp, and will squeal with delight when you take it, pull it into your mouth and bite down hard. Be patient, Kid, when those teeth of yours start coming in, they'll stop such foolishness.

I pray that your reaching and grasping will never stop, but will grow stronger each day. Whether it be for a tender-looking finger or your own toe; whether it's a reach for the hand of a loved one or for a quest placed in front of you by God, may your reach be steady and your grasp be firm. With these newly discovered skills, your life is going to be defined by the things you reach for, and the things you take hold of. In writing about wisdom and righteousness, the author of Ecclesiastes tells us in 7:18, "It is good to grasp the one and not let go of the other."

Yeah, pretty heavy stuff to take on board at this stage of your life, but I hope that one day, you'll look back over these letters and know that even now we're praying just for such things: wisdom to guide you through each day and righteousness to give it all meaning. It's never too early to start the process, and even now you're showing us that you have what it takes. Now give that toe a big bite.

TWENTY
Rocket Tests

Dear Schnicklefritz,

There comes a time in every major project when, after all systems are checked and declared ready to go, someone says, "Okay, test the engines". The image I have comes from the days of the Apollo Moon project (you'll read about it in history class); those huge Saturn Five rockets were bolted down and fired up. The earth shook for miles around, people watching from across the bay could feel the heat, and the noise was like nothing you could imagine.

But of course, it was only a test. Later on, those rockets were strapped to spaceships that carried our astronauts to the moon and back. But first everyone had to make sure they would work, first time every time.

Schnicklefritz, you're beginning to experience your own "rocket tests", and I suspect that the effect is no less awe-inspiring than feeling the heat from a Saturn Five. They're called "Braxton Hicks", and they were named after the man who wrote about them way back in 1872. He guessed correctly that this was a way for Mom's body to check the systems and make sure everything is functioning properly before the "The Big Day". We might call it a "dress rehearsal".

But that doesn't make it any less than what it is for both you and Mom. Usually, you can sense it coming before she does. You tense up, and if you could talk, you'd probably be saying something like, "Houston, we have a problem". But before you could get the message out, Mom is feeling it too: a tightening all over, growing in intensity and becoming something that definitely cannot be ignored.

But then, just when both of you are thinking, "This is it!" the sensation goes away, usually after about 20 seconds. Most of the time, Mom will recognize it for what it is, take a deep breath and wait for the moment to pass. Once in a while, especially as "B-Day" approaches, she may start thinking, "Uh, maybe this IS it!" There may even be a call to the doctor, and if she's insistent enough, even a quick trip to the ER to make sure it was only a test.

But don't worry about it, Kid; it's just another indication of what a miracle is going on all around you. You couldn't design a project like this in a million years. That's God's business, and He's got everything well in Hand. It the meantime, He's making sure you're still preparing for that moment of separation, when your world is going to come alive in ways I couldn't begin to describe. It's about this time, I hear, that your super brain is starting to take over jobs that used to come under Mom's responsibility. Your body heat, for example, used to be regulated by the amniotic fluid surrounding you. But now your brain is saying, "It's okay Mom; I've got this".

I still remember the days of the Apollo program, and I can still recall that excitement of watching all the preparations leading up to the countdown: 10, 9, 8, 7, 6, 5, 4, 3, 2, 1... But listen: what I felt back then was NOTHING compared to what I'm feeling now. Back then, it was all about sending some really brave people out into the unknown. Now, it's all about welcoming a very brave Kid into something that, while it's unknown to him, is well-known by us, and we're counting the days. 10, 9, 8, 7...

TWENTY-ONE
The Thing About Secrets

Dear Schnicklefritz,

Yesterday your grandpa and I made a trip to the mall. We do that a lot now that we're old and have some time on our hands. I don't think you, little one, will be going to the mall, at least without your mother, for many many years.

There's a reason for that. There are things at 'the mall' that you just won't be interested in for a long time. Sometimes we take your cousins and they're bored, unless of course we can end up in the pet shop or a toy store! Then they get sad because they don't have access to the money they need to take these wonders home. They don't have credit cards like we adults, so it just ends up being frustrating for them. I might mention that it can end up very wrong for us grownups, who do have those plastic cards, because sometimes they bite too, but that's another conversation for a long time from now.

What I wanted to say to you today is that I want you to give a little 'Thank you" in there to and for your Mommie.

You see, you have a mom who has a brain. She goes out of her way to take absolute pristine care of you. She's possibly at these malls right now, looking for the perfect hypoallergenic, no sharp edges, could be entirely digested with no harm to you... items. She's very careful. I've seen her hold your little clothes up to her nose, nuzzling them and imagining you're already in them.

But more than that, she's careful with her own body. She loves Jesus and will tell you all about Him, but then you probably already know a lot. She's this thing we call 'modest'. Let me explain.

One mother in particular, that we saw at the mall made us look at each other and say, "Schnicklefritz has a great mother!"

Why, you ask? This lady didn't learn any modesty at all from her mother. She walked along in a little tank top across her chest, and 'below' were tight and low yoga pants...and nothing else except the enormous stretched ball that was her stomach hanging out.

Seriously, I know you love where you're living, but it needs to be out of sight from the whole world at this point!

Rant over.

We're happy you're being kind and loving to your mom, only kicking her...well, all the time, but she can tell you mean no harm.

Psalm 139 tells us that You formed me in the SECRET place, the inmost part of my being...

TWENTY-TWO
Knowing Voices

Dear Schnicklefritz,

Well, as I mentioned the other day, you've now "gone vertical", and it looks like you're buckled in and ready to ride. In fact, I'm told that you could make your appearance at any time and be perfectly prepared. But, as with anything worth doing, something like your birthday deserves a few extra dress rehearsals. If there's any way to describe your daily routines now, it's, "Practice, practice, practice!"

All of your systems are now fully developed, but in the case of your lungs, it's a little hard to practice breathing until you get a supply of that stuff we call "air". So instead, you're inhaling and exhaling all that amniotic fluid around you. Forget what I said earlier about it being unfortunate that you have no toilet facilities, so .... well, like I said, forget it. Practice takes precedence.

It looks like you're also getting dressed to step out. That lovely transparent skin of yours is turning opaque this week. And that's good; you gotta keep some of the mystery alive, after all.

Meanwhile, you're continuing to pack on the weight, having just about doubled in size over the past month. And that means a lot of your "rocking and rolling" has been diminished to more "tapping and squirming".

But, and here's what I find fascinating: it seems obvious, and the medical people confirm it, that you're starting to distinguish things in the world around you, including the voices you're hearing through those perfect ears of yours.

Your Mom and Dad put that to the test the other day, after you had been through a particularly long sleep cycle. I mean, fair enough; you've been working hard with practice routines and probably felt you deserved a little sleep in. Nevertheless, Mom decided it was time to rise and shine. With a gentle "thump" on her belly and a whispered, "Wakie wakie", she waited and ... nothing. Once more, with a bit more force. Nothing.

Finally Dad showed up and decided to give it a go. Gentle thump, "Wakie wakie", and the response was immediate. His thump was returned at precisely the same point where it had been given. "Interesting," thought Dad. "Let's try an experiment." Moving over a few inches to another spot on the belly, he thumped, spoke, and his greeting was returned, again at the exact spot where it had been given. This continued for a while until it was evident that Dad and Schnicklefritz were having a conversation.

This does not suggest, by the way, that Mom has lost her place on the party line. On other occasions, the same experiment was carried out with her voice taking priority. But the point is, Kid, you listened, and responded differently to each voice. I couldn't help but think of Jesus' words in John 10:27, *My sheep hear my voice. I know them, and they follow me.*

It seems there is no limit to your preparations, Schnicklefritz; whether you're kickboxing, doing total submersion breathing exercises, or putting on your best Sunday-go-to-meeting skin, you're doing all that while hearing and sensing everything around you, forming proper responses and sending those signals right back.

This tells me that I'll not be surprised at all, after you're born, to find that even in the most frightening circumstances, all it will take will be a word or a touch from Mom or Dad to bring you peace and joy... just like the rest of us, when we tend to feel a little lost and alone, just a Word from the Good Shepherd is all we need.

Keep listening to your surroundings, Kid. Your folks, and that Good Shepherd, have a lot more to tell you. And so will I, just as soon as I get into earshot!

Love ya.

TWENTY-THREE
On the Wings of Eagles

Dear Schnicklefritz,

Remember what I said last time about you breathing that amniotic fluid you're floating in? I told you to forget the fact that there's no toilet in your quarters, so hopefully you've forgotten it, and don't need to think about it anymore.

...except for this one more bit of information I picked up about you this week! Breathing that fluid is very important, since it prepares those lungs for life outside, when air is going to be one of the best things you've ever experienced. But not only are your lungs in training; actually, your whole digestive system is humming away, taking in that fluid around you and processing it the same way you'll be taking Mom's milk in a few short weeks. I'm pretty sure you're going to take a drink on that day, give a burp and say, "Now that's what I'm talkin' about!"

In the meantime, keep it up, Kid. From what I hear, you're processing about a pint of fluid a day. I wonder if that's where the expression, "I'm headed down for a pint" came from?

All of that drinking and exercise is paying off in a fighting trim body. As of this week, there's more of YOU in there than there is of anything else in your surroundings. Mom is well aware of that fact, since, with the decreasing padding of fluid around you, those kicks and punches aren't hindered by anything but Mom's tummy. Be gentle, okay?

And I think you must be hearing me. More and more, it seems, you're differentiating between daytime and night-time, and, for the most part, acting accordingly. Doctors tell us that now when you're awake, those eyes are wide open and scanning in all directions. When you're asleep, they're closed and showing every sign of dream activity.

I hope you're dreaming of me, Schnicklefritz. I'm sure dreaming of you. I just can't wait until we can have some real one-on-one time together. And then someday, a few years from now, we'll sit down and look over these letters and remind ourselves of what a precious miracle you were, and still are.

It's funny, how God gives us all kinds of "life models" to help us understand our relationship with Him. I'd like to think that He's counting the days as well, anxiously waiting for the time when He and I can sit together and look back over these years when I was born again; how I learned to crawl, then to walk, to run and how I'm chomping at the bit to spread my wings and fly into His arms.

He has to tell me, just like I'm telling you: Be patient. All good things come to those who wait....*but those who wait for the LORD shall renew their strength, they shall mount up with wings like eagles, they shall run and not be weary, they shall walk and not faint. (Isaiah. 40:31)*

TWENTY-FOUR
The Village Around You

Dear Schnicklefritz,

Hello Sweetie! It's Grandma again. Today Grandpa and I made a trip from our house to yours. I think you'll especially like all the extra space, compared to what you're in now. Your Mom said that all your kicking and punching these days almost feel personal. I know it must be pretty cramped, but you're in the home stretch now!

I'm still amazed at the care you've been getting, thanks to some great parents and unbelievable technology. When I had my baby 45 years ago, things were different... or at least it seems like it.

I barely saw a doctor or got any kind of medical advice. Grandpa and I ate our way through Europe, camping and sleeping on the ground. We had no savings, no address and no real plan as to where we'd live when we got back to the States. We did know that we were headed for school in San Francisco, but beyond that, we took the Aussie attitude of "She'll be right, Mate" and let each day come as it would. We didn't even know if we were having a boy or a girl! Maybe we were just products of the hippie generation, and where everything was supposed to be 'free and easy'.

I marvel at how well you've been 'taken care' of already. Your mom sees a whole plethora of Doctors, mostly talking on the phone, (because of this little pandemic we're having at the moment), but still. Every facet of your growth and development seems to be monitored and on track. But it isn't even that. She wears what she calls a 'smart phone' which keeps a record of her pulse, and who knows what else.

To top that off, your daddy who works in the IT (think internet and technology) industry proudly announced to us that he now has the house wired to turn on lights and such just by him calling up this thing called "Alexa".

Someone has said "it takes a village" and I think your village will be just that, with heaps of loving relatives, church people and now, technology.

But I want you to always remember that the thing that hasn't changed since creation is the Very Creator who is watching over you. He always knows every breath you take, every beat of your precious little heart, and every thought you will have, both now and until the day he welcomes you back home.

Have a fun few last weeks in there. We're all scrubbing up to await your beautiful arrival!

TWENTY-FIVE
Of Dogs and Dominion

Dear Schnicklefritz,

Well, I'm told that you're just about ready for your first birthday; by that I mean, the day of your birth! Systems are up and running, muscles are toning up, lungs are fully inflated, and you even have your own immune system, ready for the day when you and your Mom will start a whole new way of relating to each other, separated on one level, but even closer on every other level. Most of the developments you're working on now are more "software related" rather than hardware, if I can use a computer term. Your brain, for example, is adding new tweaks every day, so that you'll be ready to take in all the sights and sounds that are coming your way.

And speaking of which, your Mom and Dad have started preparing Zuko for your arrival. Who is Zuko, you ask? He's the lord of the house when everyone is away, the keeper of the treasures, the protector from all threats, day or night, and until now, the object of your parents' adoration, otherwise known as the Family Dog.

...and therein lies the challenge. Believe me, Zuko is going to be your constant companion, your best playmate and your faithful bodyguard for years to come. But the problem is, he doesn't know it yet. Oh, I'm sure he has a clue that impending change is coming. He certainly spends a lot of time watching Mom's tummy when you kick and move around. With the super sense that only a dog could possess, he probably knows more details about you than any of us, even though he can't quite grasp the significance. Without that bit of crucial understanding, Zuko may not exactly welcome you with open arms at first. After all, he's about to be demoted from Alpha to Beta in the family pecking order, and he might not want to take that lying down.

So, Mom and Dad have set out on a quest to make sure Zuko accepts and loves you as quickly as possible. Step one is getting him familiarized with the idea of an addition to the family. Now, instead of just sitting together on the couch playing games and getting scratched behind his ears, Zuko is having his attention drawn to your presence, complete with words of love.

After you're born and before you come home, Dad is going to bring a blanket from your crib, fresh with your scent, and let him examine it. He will recognize at once that this carries the aroma of Mom, but something else as well… something similar but different… something that is uniquely YOU.

Then when the big day arrives, and you and Mom return home from the hospital, Zuko will be led outside to meet you on neutral ground. He'll need to understand from the start that you are part of the family and not an intruder. Then after introductions have been made all around, you and Zuko will come into the house together. I'm sure he will have lots of things to show you, and may have to be "brought down a notch" until he discovers what you can and can't do yet.

Then there will come the day when, step by step, you begin to take your rightful place as the Alpha Kid. You'll be given the chance to feed Zuko, play with him, take him for walks and when necessary, discipline him when he steps out of line. That's what people do, because that's the way God set it up, way back in Genesis 1:26, at Creation, "Then God said, 'Let us make man in our image, after our likeness. And let them have dominion over the fish of the sea and over the birds of the heavens and over the livestock and over all the earth and over every creeping thing that creeps on the earth.'"

Adam, the first man, was given the job of naming all the animals, and in keeping with that, your Mom and Dad had the task of naming Zuko. And one of these days, I expect, you'll have the job of picking a name for the next dog, cat, hamster or goldfish that comes into your household. And Zuko's going to help train you in the proper care and feeding of HIM.

So there's another project to exercise that super brain of yours, Kid. Be thinking of names you're going to give your Mom, Dad, grandparents, aunts, uncles… and Zuko. I can't wait to see what you come up with.

Grandpa.

TWENTY-SIX
That Wonderful Thumb

Hey Schnicklefritz,

Well, the excitement level around here is ramping up, as we anticipate your arrival! I'm told that your breathing exercises are becoming more regular and full-on, getting ready for that first breath of real air. There's not much room for kicking any more, but you can still move side to side, and it's become a great game lately to see where your bottom is sticking up as you try a few barrel rolls. A few more layers of fat have been added this week, as if you're packing on a little extra for the journey ahead. And speaking of food, it looks like you're getting tired of the same-old-same-old from your Mom. That thumb is in your mouth more often than not, and you're working like crazy to get that perfect fit that makes a perfect seal. I can almost hear you saying, "Come on Mom; I'm starving!!"

As you get older, "thumb sucking" might become a bit of an issue, but don't worry about it. Besides preparing for the Big Buffet, it's often an indication of stress and/or excitement. Today I caught my own thumb headed for my mouth, and just pretended like I had a hang nail. If you want to see the Thumb Sucking Pro of all time, I give you your Mother. She was a champion, able to disable any attempts at making her stop until braces finally made it impossible.

In her defence, though, she was facing a lot more stresses than (hopefully) you'll ever have to deal with. She came from a Russian orphanage, never having been outside the gate until Grandma and I showed up when she was three years old. We took her straight to America for a quick visit to family, then on to Japan where we lived and worked. Language was a huge challenge, since she spoke only Russian at first. A few weeks in America began to give her the idea that those strange sounds everyone was making meant something. But before she could start to learn anything, she found herself in Japan, where we spoke English inside the house and Japanese outside (unless of course we had Japanese friends come to visit). That's when the thumb sucking really began, poor thing! But she was a real trooper, managing her first word as the discussion came up about stopping off for something to eat on the way home. Removing her thumb from her mouth, she perked up and said, "Eat?"

Believe me Kid, you're not alone if you can feel the excitement level around here. No one's going to give you a hard time if you're restless, hungry and need a good thumb. We're all pacing, eating, and if we thought we could get away with it, sucking our thumbs. I think of the Apostle Paul, who assured us that, "… now we see in a mirror, dimly, but then we will see face to face. Now I know only in part; then I will know fully, even as I have been fully known" (1 Corinthians 13:12). Granted, he was writing about another Big Event that I look forward to telling you about when you get a little older, but the excitement and anticipation is the same. Jesus touched on it in John 16:12, when He told His disciples, "I still have many things to say to you, but you cannot bear them now."

What I'm saying, Schnicklefritz, is that all of us including you, your parents, grandparents, aunts and uncles as well as more friends than you can count are going crazy with excitement over the thought of seeing you in the flesh. That day will come soon, but in the meantime, we're just going to have to wait. And it won't stop then. Even after you're born, there will be "dance-in-a-circle-til-you-fall-down" moments when you're getting ready for the next Big Thing: first burp, first smile, first word, first step, first date…., well, you get the picture.

Let me just leave you with another tantalizing word from Brother Paul in 1 Corinthians 2:9, "But, as it is written, 'What no eye has seen, nor ear heard, nor the human heart conceived, what God has prepared for those who love him'".

Enjoy that thumb, Kid. Love ya,

Grandpa.

TWENTY-SEVEN
Welcome to the World

Dear Schnicklefritz,

The first thing I noticed about you Sunday morning was a thin scratch across your face... leftovers from some excited people helping you get born. But by evening it was just about cleared up, a testimony both to your fighting spirit and the result of all those built-in survival systems I've been reminding you of these past few months.

It seems you were ready and willing to get on with your birthday celebrations, but a combination of factors that will always be a Great Mystery to guys like me, led to a labour marathon stretching out close to 24 hours from start to finish. Thankfully you showed everyone the stuff you're made of, finally making your appearance at 1:30 am.

Mom tells me you have eyes blacker than coal (although I've heard that the colour often changes later), but that's something I'll have to observe after you've finished "sleeping it off". Everything else is just as I described it, from your super highway nervous system to that incredible beating heart tied inseparably to a set of lungs that could take the top off the hospital building. All of those things are now discreetly hidden behind layers and layers of muscle, tendons, bone and vessels all wrapped up in a perfect seal of skin that only a few days ago was translucent but now has taken on a pinkish hue.

But perhaps most telling of all was the evidence that your Mom and Dad had thought about hiding from us until the Big Reveal. Knowing the gender ahead of time is one of those experiences that I suppose will become more and more commonplace from this generation on. As a product of the last generation, I was happy to be surprised, but you know, Kid, you and I have come to know each other quite well through these letters, haven't we? I plan to print them up and keep them someplace safe until the day when the two of us can sit together and go through them one page at a time. I want you to never forget how special you are, and in fact how special you always have been, even back in those days in the "secret place" the Psalmist wrote about, when you were being knit together in love.

Gender doesn't really matter when you consider all the things I've tried to point out; that's the reason I chose "Schnicklefritz" as a temporary name for you to go by. Even when it began to come clear in my imagination, I wanted to stick with a name that would focus on Who you are and not What you are. Oh, I'm sure by the time you and I are going through these letters together, your gender will be quite important to you. This is as it should be, since it all goes together to help describe the unique properties that make you, You.

And I will never forget the day when I first laid eyes on that perfectly-knit body making up my precious grandson: But first a drum roll. The name comes from your parents' favourite verse, especially your Mom, in Jeremiah 29:11
"For I know the plans I have for you, declares the Lord, plans to prosper you and not to destroy you, to give you a hope and a future". The middle name is a shout out to my own son, your uncle, so we'll be calling you Jeremiah Nathan Pennycuick, slightly scratched but undeniably victorious, keeper of the promise of the Psalmist.

"Sons are a heritage from the Lord, children a reward from him. Like arrows in the hands of a warrior are sons born in one's youth. Blessed is the man whose quiver is full of them...."

Psalms 127:3-5 (NIV).

Between you and me, I think I'll hold on to the "Schnicklefritz" handle, just in case, one of these days, we have some secret men's business to discuss. Love ya,

Grandpa and Grandma.

FINAL THOUGHTS
The Greatest Question

When does life begin? There's a question for many a debate class, politician's lectern, doctor's office and church pulpit, not to mention middle-of-the-night musings as you lay on your bed and consider what you may have done or may be planning to do.

Some would say that life begins when that first breath is drawn, or that heart makes its first beat. Others insist that a foetus is just a foetus until he or she clears the birth canal: a matter of inches between survival and open season to anyone who wants that child to simply go away. At the extreme end of this viewpoint, there are not a few who insist that a baby's life can legally be terminated (a nice way to say "kill") even after birth. "Just lay it on the table and leave the room," one politician was recently heard to say. Another American leader, commenting on the proposal that babies who survive a failed abortion procedure should then have the right to legal protection from further attempts at termination said in an interview, "Well, that's a little extreme." Tragically, many applauded the opinions of both.

I believe that life begins at conception. You can call it old school conservativism, Bible bashing, or just plain fuddy dud, but truth is truth, no matter what box into which you try and shove it. Now I'll grant that at the end of the day, the origin of life question comes down to a faith-based decision, and that, unfortunately is not something that can be empirically proven or disproven. And so the question remains. Furthermore, people have struggled with it for centuries. Christians were some of the first to put faith into action, rescuing abandoned babies in 1st century Rome, caring for them and raising them as their own. Things like that prompted an early Roman

Emperor by the name of Julian to write, "Atheism" [the name given Christianity because it denied their gods] has been advanced by the loving treatment to strangers.... It is a scandal that the godless Galileans care not only for their own poor, but for ours as well. They love each other before they know each other."

But it is not my intention within the confines of this short book to try and convince you one way or the other. In the first place, there are a lot of theologians, apologists and medical people who can do that much better than I can. I'll leave that to the professionals.

In the second place, convincing anyone of the truth of the Gospel is not my responsibility. That honour goes to the Holy Spirit, as we can read in the Gospel of John. Jesus explains here the work of the "Advocate" (another name for "Holy Spirit", or "Comforter"), beginning in chapter 16, verse 8, "When He comes, He will prove to the world about sin and righteousness and judgement…"

So yeah, I can leave that to the professionals as well.

What does that leave for me? Simply stated, I have the freedom to enjoy my status as a child of God. I can play with other children. I can sing and dance, and paint pretty pictures that I'm sure, if God has a refrigerator in Heaven, will be stuck on the door with a magnet. I can work up a sweat doing things for my Heavenly Father, even knowing in my heart of hearts that He could certainly do those things much better than I. But I rejoice in the truth that, by God's grace, He has chosen me to do them, and I do them with all my heart, soul, mind and strength.

Sometimes it's not only sweat that I produce, but blood as well. We do live in a broken world, after all, where pain and suffering are a part of life. But when those times come, I can run to my Father, Who welcomes me with open arms, kisses my ouchies and makes me feel better.

I look back at what I just wrote and feel I need to add a word or two. If what I said seems trivial or childish... well, I suppose it is. After all, Jesus saved some His best accolades for children. "Let the little children come to me; and do not hinder them, for the kingdom of God belongs to such as these" Mark 10:14 (NIV).

And conversely, Jesus saved some His most scathing remarks for the old and wise. "I praise you, Father, Lord of heaven and earth, because you have hidden these things from the wise and learned and revealed them to little children" Matthew 11:25 (NIV).

What that says to me is that I can run to God with my hurts and with my joys, knowing that He will never turn me away. And here is a point that may need to be unpacked within a small group of trusted believers, where you can examine the multi-faceted journey of faith and discover there new ways of living a life worth the call. Ephesians 4:1 (NIV)

As you read through that beautiful passage of Scripture, do you get the same impression I do? It seems to me that, as children of God, we hold the ability to produce within our Heavenly Father moments of joy such as is felt by any parent toward a precious child. Similar thoughts are expressed all through the Bible, such as in Psalms 147:11, "The Lord delights in those who fear Him, who put their hope in His unfailing love."

Or... by our disobedience and rebellion, we have it within our grasp to cause God to suffer. Every time I refuse His love, His mercy, His salvation, God is cut to the quick, knowing the inevitable results of my refusal but unwilling to demand obedience at the cost of my free will. It takes no stretch of the imagination to feel the hurt of Jesus as He looked over the city in Luke 19:41-42, "Now as He drew near, He saw the city and wept over it, saying, 'If you had known, even you, especially in this your day, the things that make for your peace! But now they are hidden from your eyes".

Well, here I go again out onto thin theological ice. But please understand the heart from where this is coming. I believe a very, very small portion of God's relationship with me bears a resemblance to my relationship with my unborn grandchild. I know things he does not. I have a pretty good idea of what lies ahead for him, but he doesn't have a clue. His world is safe, warm and comfortable with palpable boundaries, while he is totally unaware of the bigger world out here to which he is headed. I'm excited for him and the discoveries he'll be making soon, just as I'm sure God is counting the days until I come into His Kingdom and make that amazing discovery, that all those things which have defined me until now, will on that day become insignificant by comparison.

It is my heart's prayer that you read these letters to Schnicklefritz and see there a bit of yourselves, both from the perspective of the child and that of the adult. To help facilitate that, I've added an appendix here. It's divided into 27 parts, with each part connected to the previous corresponding chapter. As you read them, imagine that it's a letter written to YOU. It's meant to be read, considered, and shared with others.

Then, as you read, may God grant you a heart to see what He wants to show you. May we all become what He has created us to be: better parents, better grandparents and better children of our Heavenly Father.

If you are so inclined, I would invite you to read each letter, one at a time, and follow up by turning back to the appropriate reference. Share each message with a group of trusted men and women and see what God might have to say to you. Happy hunting!

APPENDIX

Chapter 1 Appendix

Where does "mystery fit into your life? Do you find it frustrating when all the answers don't fall into your lap immediately? Or, is it possible that delayed revelation can add a dimension of joy to your day? Without dwelling too much on the subject (especially when it's a subject I know so little about) consider women's fashion. We all know, I hope, that clothing is not just something we wear to ward off sunburn and frostbite. Within those dresses, tank tops and short shorts, there is a modicum of modesty – and the lack thereof. Every fashion designer is facing the constant challenge of revealing just enough to catch your interest, but not so much as to overdo a good thing. And why? Because mystery plays such an important role in our lives.

But let's bring our minds back around to something more familiar. What would the wrapping paper companies do without our love of mystery? I can tell you: they'd go belly up. Christmas and birthday presents are meant to tease us with possibility. For years, I've tried to avoid talking about this, but I must make a confession. One Christmas (I think it was my ninth), my parents placed a present under the tree with my name on it. I was dying to know what it was! I begged, I pleaded, but my folks would just string me along and tell me to "be patient". Unfortunately, patience was not one of my virtues. One day while they were both out of the house, I slipped over to the Christmas tree and ever-so-carefully, peeled back the wrapping paper to see what it was. I was thrilled, but in that instant, the mystery was gone. The next few weeks before Christmas were some of the most miserable days I ever spent. When Mom and Dad would tease me about the present, I had to play along and pretend to be frustrated. Then on Christmas morning the charade continued as I tried to act surprised and excited when I finally opened the package. Without the mystery of wrapping paper, my world felt shameful and dull. And no, I won't tell you what the gift was. There has to be some element of mystery, after all.

For Schnicklefritz in the womb, it was a time of profound mystery, with each new development creating even more unknowns. I know that God could simply have given us children fully-formed and functioning. Or for that matter they could have come to us as adults, bypassing the whole infant/child/juvenile thing. Some days, I admit, the prospect has sounded inviting. But for some reason, God in His wisdom has given us the gift of growth, both in our children and in ourselves. Try to imagine all the things that have made you who you are, and then go back and trace the development of those things. When the Apostle Paul wrote in 1st Corinthians 13:12, "Now I know in part; then I shall know fully, even as I am fully known", I believe he was underscoring the blessing of mysteries revealed. The singer Michael Card once sang, "There is a joy in the journey, and a light we can love on the way". He was saying through the beauty of music that life is a mystery to be lived. Enjoy the things you learn along the way; look forward with delight to the things yet to come. God wants us to discover the mysteries around us, but in His time, not ours. Jesus hinted at that truth when He told His disciples in John 16:12, "I have much more to say to you, more than you can now bear." He was reminding them, and through them, reminding us that there is a time and place for everything. We open the wrapping paper too soon at our peril. Think about it.

Chapter 2 Appendix

When it comes to talking about names, there's certainly no lack of source material, right? There are other ways of course, but a person's name or nickname is usually the default starting point in any relationship. And our names can immediately call up both good and bad reactions. When my son was a policeman, he was sitting in a donut shop near the station (Honest! I'm not making this up). He saw what he thought was a familiar face, and so pulled out his phone and called back to the sergeant on duty. "Hey, what was the name of that guy with all the warrants?"

For the sake of protecting privacy, I'll use "Fred". Hanging up the phone, my son called out, "Hey Fred?"

"Yeah?" the man answered.

"Sorry to ruin your day, but we're going to jail."

The Bible has plenty to say about a person's name. Remember Proverbs 22:1? "A good name is more desirable than great riches"

I think we all recognize what my son has learned from everyday experience, that is, when a person's good name is besmirched, it's a long and torturous trail before that name is restored. On the other hand, anyone with a good name and reputation can find both snatched away in a heartbeat.

I may have done my grandkid a disservice by attaching such a name as Schnicklefritz. Even though it won't (hopefully!) be the one on his/her birth certificate. Once it gets out, that's sure to open doors to all kinds of teasing. But I pray it will be a reminder to us all to take our names seriously. Wear them with pride and use them to achieve great things.

Think about it.

Chapter 3 Appendix

There's a point in this letter that I need to reiterate, because a lot of life's choices are based on it. I'm referring of course to our emotions. All too often, when logic fails us and trusted counsellors are few and far between, those times when decisions need to be made, the thing we fall back on is how we feel about the situation. "Just follow your heart." Or, in the words of our 60's era gurus, "If it feels good, do it."

Okay, I confess to taking a bit of ministerial license when I used Schnicklefritz's emerging heartbeat and pulled a sermon point from it, but hey, it's what I do. And as I said at the beginning, it's a point that needs making.

So how can we make solid decisions when solid facts are in short supply? First of all, you can do what I hope you're doing right now: bounce your quandaries off a small group of men and women whose faith you can trust. There is such a thing as the "corporate will of God", and that simply means allowing a group of people to think and pray about an issue and see how God directs the group. I hate to say it, but all of us at one time or another can be mistaken in our understanding of God's will, and that underscores the importance of having our understanding tested against the group. This would have come in very handy for a colleague of mine who determined that it was God's will for him to divorce his wife and run off with the pianist.

And that unfortunate situation brings up the other point I'd like to make when it comes to heart decisions: test everything against God's Word as found in the Bible. If what you're contemplating contradicts what God has said, then it's probably wrong. Think about it.

Chapter 4 Appendix

I've picked up on the fact that quite a few people in the world today equate "work" with "punishment". Have you ever seen prisoners in bright orange coveralls along the side of the road, picking up garbage? And what did you think? Yeah, they did something bad and now they're being punished for it.

Or, have any of you been sent to detention after school? Usually there's work involved, even if it's nothing more than pulling staples out of papers or sweeping the floor... at least that's what I've been told.

But the surprising thing we discover in Genesis is that work was a thing in the Garden of Eden, even before sin came in and broke things. Adam was told to give names to every animal. That was an important job, by the way; just refer back to the chapter on names and the relationships that come from them. And I think Adam enjoyed his work. He had a sense of accomplishment and could go to bed at night knowing that the world was a better place. It wasn't until sin crept in like a train wreck that a new dimension to work was added: sweat.

"By the sweat of your brow you will eat your food until you return to the ground..." Genesis 3:19 (NIV).

So it is what it is. Sometimes work is hard, and sadly sometimes it's not all that fulfilling. But the Bible tells us over and over that work is good, and not a thing to be avoided. Look at Paul's admonition to the folks in Thessalonica.

"… aspire to live quietly, and to mind your own affairs, and to work with your hands, as we instructed you, so that you may walk properly before outsiders and be dependent on no one"

1 Thessalonians 4:11-12 (NIV).

"But Jesus answered them, "My Father is working until now, and I am working" John 5:17 (NIV).

Even Schnicklefritz has his work cut out for him, and it's not always easy. I believe with all my heart, even if God called him home today, that child would still hear the words of his Creator,

"Well done, good and faithful servant! You have been faithful with a few things; I will put you in charge of many things. Come and share your master's happiness!" Matthew 25:23 (NIV).

Chapter 5 Appendix

With all the focus on birth and life and the joy that comes with babies, maybe it seems a little out of place to bring up the subject of death. But I think it's appropriate here because of the analogies we're given in the two experiences.

Doesn't it seem to you that God is giving us lots of "object lessons" taken from our daily lives, and applying them to things that will someday make a huge difference to each of us in a personal way? Jesus did it all the time, and we call them "parables". I find it fascinating that we refer to God as "Father" and as Christians, to each other as brother and sister; then we're given the chance to illustrate that wonderful truth through the family unit. Sadly, we don't always get it right, and I shudder to think of Jesus' observation about what to do with those who put stumbling stones in front of children. See Mark 9:42, above.

But it's just impossible to ignore the birth of a baby and not draw comparisons to the death experience. For all that child knows, he is dying. Everything that defined his life up to that moment is taken from him, and the "terror face" comes quite naturally. But looking around that scene, we see nothing but smiles and laughter and encouragement. And that's because we know that birth is a happy thing.

Personally, I can't wait to see what kind of reception I'm going to get when my time comes to leave this life. I'm no saint, and I'm pretty sure there will be a lot of fear and uncertainty on my part, in spite of the faith I've staked my life on. But that time of doubt will dissolve away the moment I see the smiling face of Jesus. Of course, I can't say all this without considering the alternative.

Romans 8:28 (NIV) assures us that... *"in all things God works for the good of those who love Him, who have been called according to his purpose."* But the assurance doesn't apply to those who don't know Him. For those, all things will work together for bad. Think about it.

Chapter 6 Appendix

Hopefully, I'm preaching to the choir here when I mention the importance of listening. And how appropriate is it that the gift of hearing comes to a child before seeing and speaking! We've all heard the stories, I'm sure, of people who did not have that gift, and how they overcame their difficulties in miraculous ways.

Do you know that wonderful story of Helen Keller? As an infant, she was struck blind and deaf, destined it seemed to spend her life alone, surrounded only by the pity of all who saw her. But by God's grace, she was rescued by a teacher, Anne Sullivan, who taught her to spell using a system of touching. Reading about her accomplishments never fails to inspire and serves as yet another reminder that relationships begin with what we hear, or sense, as the case may be. Our response to that stimulus opens a door to life that might never be realized by any other way.

Awesomely appropriate then, are the words of Jesus in John 15:16, *"You did not choose me, but I chose you and appointed you so that you might go and bear fruit..."*.

Think about it.

Chapter 7 Appendix

"Evolution" versus "Creationism" is not a soapbox I plan to stand on in this book, but when it comes to the unborn, there are just some things that can't be ignored. From that perch, we hear words like "irreducible complexity", and in the case of Schnicklefritz's eyes, there are no better words to describe them. How could blind chance develop a complex system such as sight, complete with focus, colour and exposure control? And don't fall for that "poor design" complaint; it's long been debunked by scientists a lot smarter than the person who wrote it. And then when everything required for sight is completed, that system is carefully protected until the time it's needed. Just like those deciduous trees needing protection from the coming winter, God has planned in a whole world of checks and balances just for our benefit.

And it's all there in order to give us the best possible chance of seeing and appreciating all that He's put together. How true the words, *"The heavens declare the glory of God; the skies proclaim the work of His hands"* Psalms 19:1 (NIV).

Think about it.

Chapter 8 Appendix

Not long ago, I read where a murder was solved when some leaves in the trunk of a car were determined through DNA testing to have come from a particular tree in a nearby park where the crime had been committed. My first response was No Way! Then I learned that, Yes Way, every tree, every plant, every animal and every human has its own unique DNA signature. This is God's way of placing His mark on His creation.

That's quite a good comeback to those who try to tell me I'm just an insignificant speck in a meaningless universe. And a great comfort when I think of Satan trying to claim me as his own, and hearing the voice of God saying, "Look again; that child is Mine."

I'm reminded of Colossians 1:19-20(NIV), where I'm reminded that "...*God was pleased to have all His fullness dwell in Him, and through Him to reconcile to Himself all things, whether things on earth or things in heaven, by making peace through His blood, shed on the cross.*"

I've often used this verse, by the way, to assure folks that yes, all dogs go to Heaven. I then carry that on to the obvious conclusion that the only exceptions to that statement are those, who by the gift of freewill, choose not to accept God's offer of love and forgiveness. That raises the question, of course: are there "bad dogs" who miss the cut? Well, that's a question for those theologians with more time on their hands. I'll leave it alone, but ... think about it.

Chapter 9 Appendix

Of all the systems in the world today, I think the ones that involve communication are among the most important, ever. In the case of Schnicklefritz, it's absolutely essential today, as nerve pathways are being established that will enable him to accomplish everything from breathing to walking to becoming the next Prime Minister.

For you and me, without the ability to communicate, we'd be drifting, unable to live or love, or most importantly, to make contact with our Creator. And isn't it fitting then, that God has made us with so many ways to reach out beyond ourselves? From our facial expressions, to body language, to words and language, all the way to a heart level that only God knows.

This has been one source of comfort I've been able to share with those whose loved ones slip away without ever coming to that Romans 10:9 experience of *"confessing with your mouth that Jesus is Lord"*. As Christians, we have pointed to that physical act as the pathway to salvation, and as a pastor I believe and preach that truth. But I'll allow the possibility that God has ways of communicating with His children about which I know nothing. And this is why I can offer hope to those who grieve, insisting that we may never know this side of Heaven what went on between God and the Dearly Departed before the actual departure.

Think about it.

Chapter 10 Appendix

I'd like us to consider again the sacrifices our mothers make for us, even if at times they're not aware of it. I've already mentioned the supply line we call the umbilical cord, and how the baby gets first pick of everything necessary for life. Then if there's anything left over, it goes to Mom. It's fascinating to watch as a mother-to-be will stand, talking to friends or waiting for a bus, with her hands on her "baby bump", patting and rubbing. Having not experienced that myself, I can only speculate. Help me out, Moms. Yeah, she's going through a lot of physical discomfort, but I believe she's also sensing the need, even unconsciously, to love on that baby, saying as only she can, "I'm here, Sweetie. You're okay."

And there is an even stronger manifestation of that need. I was moved to tears, but not particularly surprised to hear my son say on the day his son was born, "It's amazing, Dad; suddenly I have this undeniable feeling that if necessary, I'd gladly die for him right now."

That's a gift from God, and in the natural scheme of things, the gift shows itself in every mother and father on the planet. It's only among those who have been mortally wounded by the enemy of this world that we don't see that altruistic nature.

And remember what I said earlier about the everyday things in this life showing us Divine truths? Where else do we see such a willingness to sacrifice one's life for an other, even one who by virtue of youth, ignorance or downright rebellion fails to recognize his or her part in the sacrifice?

Think about it.

Chapter 11 Appendix

I hope I'm not overstating the obvious here, but every week I get new reminders about my Creator. It's often been said, especially during times of impatient waiting, that God is "sometimes slow, but never late". I think of Schnicklefritz, and the amount of time that has to pass from conception to birth. I can almost see him, squirming around in his world that's getting more cramped every day. If he had the ability to be impatient (which thankfully I believe hasn't come yet), I could almost hear him saying, "Look, I've got ears. I've got eyes. I've got lungs. I've got a central nervous system. Let's get on with it!"

Such imaginations come easily, because I've been guilty of the same attitude, over and over again. I've got my ideas about how things should be going, and what should be happening next. But the more I complain to God, the more I can sense His smiling face, and His words of gentle rebuke. "Not yet, Tony; not yet." And the more I hear those words, the more frustrated I become. "Why? WHY do I have to wait?"

I was reminded this week that, in spite of all the awesome progress Schnicklefritz has made in his development, he's only halfway to his appointed delivery day. If he were to make the scene right now, it would probably end tragically, because there are still things to be accomplished.

Back in my last year of high school, I fell head over heels in love. She was beautiful. She was smart. She was everything I imagined the perfect wife could be. And I was making plans. In a few short months, I would be graduating, after which I would find a great job that paid at least minimum wage.

I had a car, and the high octane in that engine was nothing compared to the testosterone burning through my system. I think you know what I mean.

And she felt the same way, at least up to a point. I think you know what I mean. And when it started to become obvious that my plans for love and marriage were not going to come together for a while at least, I cried out, "Why? WHY do I have to wait?" The answer came with the passage of time. I got a little older, a little smarter, and a little better equipped to handle life and all the things that were about to start raining down on me.

And then I met Marsha. We ticked all the right boxes, made all the right preparations, and then one day God smiled down on us and said, "Okay kids; it's time." That was fifty-five years ago at the time I write this, and not a day goes by that I don't thank God for His wisdom, and for making me wait.

How did the psalmist put it? *"Wait for the Lord; be strong and take heart and wait for the Lord"* (Psalms 27:14 NIV).

Think about it.

Chapter 12 Appendix

When we moved into our home in Australia, we had just retired after forty years of missionary service. It was a huge effort, coupled with the closing down of our parents' estates, that finally enabled us to gather up and bring to our new home everything we owned. There were boxes we had packed up when we first left for Africa in 1973 that had never been opened since then. When we finally settled into our place and started going through things, I experienced something that's difficult to describe. Everywhere I looked, I saw history! I'm sure there's no word for the interior design one would see in our house. Nothing matches, and without a docent to serve as guide, there would be no way for a visitor to properly "visit". Every item in the living room has a story, and while Marsha and I find them fascinating, I'm sure our guests must endure a lot for their cup of coffee.

My office is the worst. Finally, enough shelf space to unpack and set up things the way I'd dreamed of doing for years! It's a wonder I get anything done; no sooner would an idea start to formulate than I'd look up and see a rock I found lying at the base of the Great Wall of China, or my Grandmother's diary, or a piece of melted plastic, remains of a pay phone I had used to call Marsha just before the building I was in exploded and burned to the ground. How could I ever hope to think lofty thoughts when surrounded by so much Past?

But that's the point I wanted to make to Schnicklefritz in this letter, and I hope to discuss it with him some day face to face. Memories begin very early in all of us, even before we are born. A collection of memories make up what we call history. And history is what makes us... well... Us!

All of our history is not necessarily pleasant to recall, but I think God allows us to hold it because, in part, recalling our past helps us better frame our future. I shudder to think what would happen if those who preach "Cancel Culture" succeed in removing the building blocks upon which our generation has been set. I think it was George Santayana who wrote back in 1905, "Those who cannot remember the past are condemned to repeat it."

When you have a suitable time and place, sit back and recollect the people, places and events that make up your own history.

Then think about it.

Chapter 13 Appendix

I've counselled a lot of young couples over the years. Now that I think about it, the majority of the serious counselling sessions were not necessarily with the young. Kids can have issues that stem mostly from, how shall I say? "kid stuff". Emotions gone wild, doubts about faithfulness, hormones misdirected. These can be quite serious, to be sure, but just as young people in love can go way overboard in times of trouble, they can also move quickly back to centre, and then enjoy that wonderful experience of "making up".

Sometimes, all I need to do is listen while they tell me what the problem is, sip my coffee while they explain what they need to do, then give them a big hug and a "you're welcome" when they tell me how much I've helped.

But a lot of the problems I've come across, the ones that keep me awake at night, involve older, more "mature" couples. These are the men and women who are no longer driven by raging hormones but have settled into a quiet, comfortable relationship with each other. These are the old folks you see at the restaurant, sitting together and eating in silence, each one knowing exactly what the other is thinking, or at least they pretend to. These are the couples who are often admired from a distance; the ones that give a picture to the old romantic declaration, "Let's grow old together."

And so it comes as a shock when people like this, in times of real honesty, confess that they're miserable. And the problem? Communication has ceased, and each has descended into his or her own private world where nothing is shared. The husband, when confronted, will insist, "She knows I love her; I don't have to tell her every day!" Yes, you do, Sir. Now, even more than ever, as age creeps up, and fears and doubts become more the norm than the oddity. She is desperate to hear that there is still one bit of solid ground to cling to: to know that she is loved. I could go on, but I hope you get the picture. Even before birth, Schnicklefritz needs to know that he is loved, even though he can't express it yet. That's the way God made us, after all. We are His children, held together by the common bonds of faith, acceptance and a love that needs to grow daily. And we can't do that in isolation. We really do need each other. Think about it, then do something about it.

Chapter 14 Appendix

I must share something that a man once told me. The story has stayed with me because he was one of the greatest men I've ever known. His name was Naoki Noguchi and, believe it or not, he was a former Kamikaze pilot in World War II. I'd love to tell you all about him, but that would be a different book. In fact, it is a book you can find on Amazon called, "Sacrificed: Given to an Empire, Found by God". But enough of that; here's the point I want to make.

We were talking one day about what in the world would lead a 15-year-old boy to decide to become a Kamikaze. The talk came around to authority, and I've had to mull that over a lot since then. Naoki said to me, "Look at a kite up in the sky. Flying up in the clouds, like a bird. Surely that's a picture of perfect freedom. But look closer: stretching from that kite to the ground is a long string, gripped by the Kite Master. As long as he holds the string tightly, the kite flies and puts on a magnificent show. But as soon as the Kite Master releases his grip on the string, it never ends well.

"As a young Japanese boy, I needed that authority. I needed it so much, that even death took a back seat. Today as a Christian, I still need the Kite Master. But I can see now that He's neither a parent, nor a teacher nor even an Emperor. He's God, my Creator and the One Whom I can trust for all eternity."

Schnicklefritz is beginning to learn, even now, that there are limits to his freedom. And the process will continue after he is born, becoming more and more painful as he makes his demands known. That's where we can do him a great service by showing him how much better life can be when we live under authority. And not just any authority. He needs to understand that there are a lot of applicants out there for the job of holding his strings, but only One Who can do it correctly.

Whoever you are and whatever your circumstance today, I can guarantee that you are never far from someone in need of wise counsel. Think about that, then look around.

Chapter 15 Appendix

Australians have a great way to describe a mother-to-be. The word is "clucky". If you've spent any time around chickens, then I'm sure you get the picture. When the time for birth draws near, everyone joins in the fun.

I've just learned that in South Africa, a Baby Shower is called a 'Stork `party`. Whatever it's called, underlying all the food and frivolity, there is a message that everyone can hear loud and strong: "There's a baby on the way, and we're going to make sure he or she has a proper home." Gifts come from all directions, all designed to insure the comfort and safety of the newborn. Diapers, outfits, blankets and toys in abundance line the baby's first abode like feathers in a bird's nest. On a more subtle, but at least as important level, mother is encouraged through the laughter. Rest assured there will be no lack of advice covering everything from the birth itself to expected effects on the home and everyone in it. Through all these celebrations, a nest is coming together, woven by the skills of countless generations, and made as comfortable as only a mother can make it. From the moment that child is carried into the nursery, she knows that she is home. This is part of the Divine model we're given, and which this book talks about from beginning to end.

Knowing that fact makes the words of Jesus in Matthew 8:20 all the more poignant. *"Foxes have dens and birds have nests, but the Son of Man has no place to lay his head."*

With the mission Jesus came to fulfill, there was neither time nor opportunity to have a home, but it seems obvious that He desired one. When the disciple, Peter, reminded Him that *"We have left everything to follow you"* (Mark 10:29 NIV), Jesus must have felt the ache in Peter's heart, and was quick to reassure him in the next verse, *"Truly I tell you, no one who has left home or brothers or sisters or mother or father or children or fields for me and the gospel will fail to receive a hundred times as much in this present age: homes, brothers, sisters, mothers, children and fields – along with persecutions – and in the age to come eternal life…"*

I take great joy knowing that Schnicklefritz is coming into a home that has been lovingly prepared for him. It breaks my heart to think of those who are missing that blessing. But God's Word assures me that even those can look forward to a heavenly home which is too wonderful to be imagined. My question to you, Dear Readers, is this: what are you doing to ensure that our children today have access to a love-lined nest, and moreover that all of us can know what home has been prepared for God's children? Think, and pray about it.

Chapter 16 Appendix

That word, "dream" is probably one of the most used and least understood part of the English vocabulary. A good-looking girl can be referred to as a "dreamboat". When the Aussies say, "You're dreamin!" that's another way of suggesting that you might be a couple of eggs short of a dozen. Martin Luther King, Jr. said in a speech now become famous, "I have a dream", and no one was about to suggest that he was lazy and spent too much time sleeping.

Right now, I want to focus on Jacob's son, Joseph. Now there's a great study on parenting and sibling relationships! In Genesis 37:19, his brothers saw him approaching and said to each other, *"Here comes that dreamer!"* And once again, they were not describing Joseph as lazy or addled-brained. When you look at the story closely, you can see that those young men were actually afraid of Joseph. He had been making some pretty off-the-wall statements about his future relationships with his brothers, his parents, even with the Jewish people as a whole. And all those revelations, he insisted, came to him in dreams. These prophecies (and as it turned out, they were just that), would affect those brothers in ways they desperately wanted to avoid, even if it meant fratricide.

Among a wealth of other great morals to this story, the one that strikes close to my heart is the idea that God can and does speak to His people in dreams. Try this as a Bible study sometime: look for every instance where Scripture shows us people being led by dreams. Nearly every night before I go to sleep, I pray, "Lord, do You have anything to tell me while I sleep? Give me ears to hear with. Please."

I have to admit, I can't claim any "Joseph-type" dreams, but there was at least one time, following the death of my son, when God gave me a colour by technicolour look at the event, showing me perspectives, I never would have seen on my own. I normally dream in black and white, by the way. This one was high definition. As a result, even though I still can't say this was a ministry tool I would have chosen, I was left with the assurance that, one of these days, my son and I will stand together and declare, "Thank You, Lord, for that valley You took us through!" Not ready to say that today, mind you, but some day.

In the meantime, let's not diminish the power of dreams. I believe this is often one of the best ways God can get through to us. And I believe it starts at a very early age, right Schnicklefritz?

Think about it.

Chapter 17 Appendix

When Marsha and I were first married, life was tough, but the ideals we clung to were easy. Our friends might be sinking into perma debt, but we would never be so irresponsible. While we managed it for the most part, we were given a credit card by Tony's employer, and a couple of years later when we got it paid off, finally, we'd learned some valuable lessons.

But our kids, now, that was non-negotiable! All around us, we'd see the children of our peers moving into circles they shouldn't have been moving. And when the consequences of those decisions became apparent, Marsha and I would look at each other with all-knowing eyes and whisper, "Yep; saw that one coming."

Make no mistake: when our children came along, they would never fall victim to such snares. And why, you ask? Because they would be led, gently but firmly along the right path by parentals who were possessed with the wisdom of the saints.

Fast forward a few years. We had children of our own. We began to discover that those kids had something called "personalities". Marsha and I pictured tiny little gremlins, running rampant through our children's brains, forcing them into places where they had no business, then clouding their minds with some kind of "common sense clouder" (CSC) that rendered them incapable of rational thought.

This theory was backed up as we began to see other children falling off the rails for no explainable reason at all. And the terrifying thing was that the parents of these children were just like us! They loved their kids. They exercised justice and discipline exactly as we would have. And in spite of all their best efforts, the parents seemed to have no control over the decisions their wayward offspring made. Now when Marsha and I look at each other, an old expression comes to mind: "There but for the grace of God, go I."

Before I go farther, let me say, our kids to this point have been "full of grace". Yeah, they've made a few choices that we might not have made, and sometimes they turn out good, and sometimes they have paid the price for them, but I think one factor for which I will always be grateful is the assurance that they have never doubted the fact that they are loved. This is not to say that at some point in the future they won't stumble, but then I could say the same thing about myself. I must be aware when those feelings of pride start to overshadow reality. The enemy of this world never takes a holiday, and is constantly looking, probing, searching for any weakness that he can exploit. And once in a while, he succeeds, and for no other reason that he's dealing with that part of God's Creation in possession of a personality. Because of our "personhood", we have choices. Some are better than others, some can be downright soul-destroying. But God, in His love and mercy, will not prevent us from making those choices, because to do so would be to remove our freedom.

So what I said to Schinicklefritz I say to us all: thank God for the personality that sets you apart. Use that for the glory of God, and don't let Satan get his hands on it. And if, by some chance, he does manage to get a grip, look to those fellow believers around you for help and support. Let them pray for you. Listen to what they have to say.

And think about it.

Chapter 18 Appendix

I love the image Marsha gave us of those Egyptian hieroglyphics and the suggestion that there are some who believe folks back then always walked around with their arms akimbo and their faces turned to one side. I don't believe those early Egyptians had not yet discovered how to draw a three-dimensional picture; how could they have ever built the pyramids using two-dimensional blueprints? Perhaps it was simply a matter of logistics, doing their best with the materials they had to work with. Try telling a story in pictures by writing on a rock with a paintbrush!

But it is a fact that we live according to what we know, or don't know, as it were. The people in Mary Shelly's day honestly believed that, given just the right charge of electricity, it might possible to bring the dead to life. So the story of Frankenstein's monster was perfectly plausible.

And to a certain extent, the same can be said of us today. Before 3D imaging came around, an unborn baby was not quite "real" in our minds, making it easier to discount and thus question "its" right to exist. Truth has not changed, but our perception of the truth is being challenged on a daily basis, thanks in part to 3D imaging. Knowledge is another great way to polish one's perception. As Paul said in 2 Timothy 2:15, *"Do your best to present yourself to God as one approved, a worker who does not need to be ashamed and who correctly handles the word of truth."*

Think about it.

Chapter 19 Appendix

When I attended Colorado State University (about a hundred years ago, it seems), we had a school newspaper that went by the name, "Reach". Under the title was a familiar quote by Robert Browning, "Ah, but a man's reach should exceed his grasp, or what's a heaven for?" Come to think of it, I strongly suspect that if the newspaper is still around, it's been rendered politically correct by replacing "man's" with "person's", and of course the word "heaven" has been struck because it smacks of Christianity.

But let's be reasonable; I hope we're not so misogynistic that we can accept the term "man" as referring to human beings in general. And whether a man believes in it or not, the concept of "heaven" is one that calls us to perfection, striving to attain righteousness in an unrighteous world. When Schnicklefritz reaches out for the impossible, we may laugh at his efforts, but that desire to grasp is a trait we admire in anyone, and in fact marks the real heroes of any generation.

When Jesus instructs us in Matthew 5:48(NIV) to *"Be perfect, therefore, as your heavenly Father is perfect"*, He wasn't kidding. We are to strive for perfection in every aspect of our lives. We may not achieve that goal in this lifetime, but the striving will make us better people.

I've always been inspired, and I imagine that this applies to you as well, by the unforgettable words of the prophet in Isaiah 40:31(NIV), *"... but those who hope in the Lord will renew their strength. They will soar on wings like eagles; they will run and not grow weary, they will walk and not be faint."*

The image I've always had is of a huge jetliner racing down the runway. Its mighty engines are straining against the brakes, eager to take to the sky. When it's released, it moves forward, slowly but surely overcoming its huge mass that holds it back. Faster and faster it goes until it reaches lift-off speed. The pilot pulls back on the yoke and the plane breaks free to soar, grasping for the heights.

A great image, but a lifetime of experience and a careful reading of the passage suggests to me that my understanding has been backwards. Look again: the scene is not walking, running then soaring, but rather the reverse. Soaring, running...then walking. Let's face it, when you're with Jesus, soaring comes as naturally as breathing. *"Lord, it is good for us to be here. If you wish, I will put up three shelters – one for you, one for Moses and one for Elijah"* Matthew 17:4 (NIV).

But what was true for Peter is true also for us. We were not made to live on the mountaintop. The strength that comes from faith in Christ is not fully comprehended when we're soaring with the eagles, but rather when we find ourselves in the valley. Struggling to live as a child of God among the mundane, or farther down yet in the midst of grief. Those are the times, and I speak from experience, when flying or even running is out of the question. When your world seems so shattered that it threatens to crush you where you stand. But stand you do, lifted up by the strong arms of your heavenly Father. In times like those, your reach indeed seems to exceed your grasp. But just like Schnicklefritz, reaching beyond the sphere of possibility to grasp something he cannot yet understand, children of faith reach out to the Mystery. And the Mystery calls back.

Think about it.

Chapter 20 Appendix

As missionaries to Japan, Marsha and I have participated in many tea ceremonies. Called "ochakai", or sometimes, "chado", they are just what the word means: a celebration of tea. But to a traditional Japanese person, the occasion consists of so very much more. Historically, a proper ochakai can mean the difference between divorce and marriage between couples, war and peace between countries and divine enlightenment between a man and his creator. I've known people who have completed doctorate degrees built upon nothing more than the intricacies of this simple yet profound celebration over a cup of tea.

And the beauty of this celebration lies in the degree of preparation that goes into it. The way you enter the room, the words that are spoken, the way you sit. There's even strict attention given to the way you receive the cup: take it in both hands, turn it three times, comment about it, then drink precisely three times, making sure you empty it, complete with a ladylike but audible slurp. I'm no scholar when it comes to ochakai, but it seems that the driving motivation is to perform the ceremony absolutely perfectly. In so doing, you have demonstrated your commitment to the occasion.

How does this relate to the birth process, and by association, to you and me? As I said earlier, God in His wisdom has given us a world of instructions for living, packaged up in the familiar, in order to prepare us for the Mystery to come.

A farmer sowing seed, a fisherman casting a net, a woman weaving a cloth, a young man courting a young woman, a baby preparing to be born. All these things teach us how to be children of God. Just as Schnicklefritz is preparing for life beyond what he now knows, you and I are being given the opportunity to get ready for that next Great Chapter. In the process, we will begin to see what the Bible has been teaching us all along: leaving this world is nothing less than going home.

Think about it.

Chapter 21 Appendix

As I'm sure you've seen, the bulk of these letters tries to focus on Schnicklefritz's development and how it shows us so wonderfully how amazing God is, and how He is doing so much to show us that He loves us and has a special plan and place just for us in His perfect scheme of things. What has not been so obvious, perhaps, is the view from the other side. Given that we are His loved and precious creation, does that mean that we have a responsibility to live by certain standards that honour Him? The Apostle Paul broached the subject in Romans 13:13 (NIV) with the reminder, *"Let us behave decently, as in the daytime, not in carousing and drunkenness, not in sexual immorality and debauchery, not in dissension and jealousy."* And his message was not just for the Romans. The church at Ephesus, and by association, all Christians everywhere were told clearly, *"But among you there must not be even a hint of sexual immorality, or of any kind of impurity, or of greed, because these are improper for God's holy people. Nor should there be obscenity, foolish talk or coarse joking, which are out of place, but rather thanksgiving"* Ephesians 5:3-4 (NIV).

I could go on, but I think you get the picture. There is indeed a particular lifestyle associated with the believer, a way of living that sets him or her apart from the rest of the world. Putting that into practice has given Christians an image of foolishness, weakness and ignorance, to which I might simply quote Brother Paul once again. *"We are fools for Christ"* I Corinthians 4:10 (NIC), *"But God chose the foolish things of the world to shame the wise...,"* and he continues, *"God chose the weak things of the world to shame the strong"* I Corinthians 1:27 (NIV)."

As to ignorance, that is a different matter. Believers might appear ignorant because they lack a working knowledge of many of the things the world considers important. But the

Bible reminds us that we are not to be ignorant of the things that count. Between the two of them, Apostles Paul and Peter reiterate at least six times that God's people are to be "in the know" when it comes to living as we should. Marsha pointed out in this letter that a person's life on the outside is a reflection of what he believes on the inside. So yes, we are to be modest, moral and upright, not just because it's good for society, but because it's part of the decree under which we live.

Unfortunately for Schnicklefritz, such attributes do not always come naturally. Even a child has to be taught what is proper and decent, and the job of teacher has been given to we adults.

Think about it.

Chapter 22 Appendix

I can't hear the word, "shepherd" without remembering our friend, Kumiko, back in Japan. She and her husband, Shinkichi, gave us the best introduction to Japan than we could have ever hoped for. From language, to culture, to the proper care and feeding of our church, they were truly sent by God. Then Kumiko got sick. By that time, Marsha and I had been transferred to Bangkok in order to work with the Japanese there. We were devastated, and when we were told that she had only hours left, we jumped on a plane and raced for Japan.

Just before we arrived, she slipped into a coma as her family stood around her bedside. As they prayed together, Kumiko's eyes suddenly flew open. She sat straight up, and with a huge grin on her face, she exclaimed, "Oh look! Shepherds!" With that, she lay back down and slipped peacefully into the arms of Jesus.

I've got a lot of questions when I get to Heaven, but I think one thing is pretty clear from this experience. As God's children, we have absolute assurance of His Presence and Protection. "… God has said, 'Never will I leave you; never will I forsake you'." Schnicklefritz is learning even now to distinguish between the voices coming within earshot. Furthermore, he's learning to pick out the voices that bring him comfort. Speaking of life lessons, John 10:14 (NIV) says, *"I am the good shepherd; I know my sheep and my sheep know me"*. Can you think of a time when you were comforted by something or someone familiar to you?

Think about it and share it with a friend.

Chapter 23 Appendix

The thing that impressed me this week about Schnicklefritz's development is that so many of his systems are coming together and ready to be put to work, although so far, those systems have no opportunity for testing.

The eyes, for example, are geared up for seeing, but they're still sealed up tight until just before he's born and brought into the light. His lungs are built to breathe, but today all he can manage is a lungful of amniotic fluid.

I've mentioned this before, but isn't it amazing how God is giving us models today that will prepare us for life tomorrow? I like to compare it to that state-of-the-art stereo system that will reproduce sounds the human is incapable of hearing.

I saw a man last year driving his high-end Ferrari down Hawaii's crowded H1 interstate highway (the only one of four highways, and it's only 27 miles long). The poor man looked miserable! Here he was, in a state-of-the-art machine capable of going 0- 62 in 2.9 seconds, yet all he could manage was 35 mph with cars and trucks on all sides.

What do you suppose God has in store for us? I can only imagine, and even that will come up short, because 1 Corinthians 2:9 (NIV) reminds me that if I can conceive it, then that's not what God has prepared, since, well, since I can't conceive it.

In the meantime, like Schnicklefritz, I'm going to use what I have to help me prepare for those future experiences. What things do you possess that so far at least, you're unable to fully utilize? How will those things help you when the time finally comes, and God tosses you the keys and says, "Okay, Child, open 'er up!"

Chapter 24 Appendix

It wasn't very long ago when all our Bible study groups struggled with some of the miraculous things we read, unable to comprehend how such things would look. Take the Second Coming of Christ, for example. How could one event be seen simultaneously by everyone in the world? But there it is, in Revelation 1:7 (NIV), *"Look, he is coming with the clouds"*, and *"every eye will see him, even those who pierced him...."* This seems to suggest a single event that is witnessed not only by everyone at the same time, but also something that will include every generation. We may not have learned how to do time travel yet, but with a few satellites and a lot of receivers, we just might be able to pull off a global telecast.

Then there's that "mark of the beast thing", where something physical placed on your body can be connected to a worldwide web. *"... it also forced all people, great and small, rich and poor, free and slave, to receive a mark on their right hands or on their foreheads, so that they could not buy or sell unless they had the mark..."* Revelation 13:16-17 (NIV). I don't think I need to unpack that one for you.

Before, our Bible study groups finally had to conclude that God is God, His ways are not our ways, and just accept that His Word is true even if we can't comprehend it. And of course, that's still the case today. While modern technology might help us imagine some of the miraculous things we read, it in no way explains them. Sadly, a lot of people I meet simply will not accept the Bible because they can't accept the idea of miracles. I try to explain that God, by His Nature, stands outside of His creation, and is not bound by a single law of nature. If He wants to part the Red Sea, make a shadow go backwards or turn water into wine, that is entirely His prerogative. If He was unable to do those things, then by definition He would not be God.

Schnicklefritz lies before us as an absolute embodiment of God's miraculous power at work. Looking at the ways man has tried to copy the technology can only convince us that we cannot even come close. Robots are fascinating inventions but only a science fiction writer could make them into something human. It's recently been suggested that some of the Artificial Intelligence devices out there are becoming sentient, that is knowing that they exist; and while they play a mean game of chess and can whip out math problems that would take us years, most of us would agree that it's a far cry from what even a baby like Schnicklefritz can do in his sleep.

I'm not sure who first coined the phrase, "it takes a village", but when it first started spreading, no one could possibly imagine what that village would look like today. So let's enjoy the technology that is making our lives easier, and in some ways, safer, but let no one suggest that we are developing beyond our need for God. No village can long be sustained without His Hand over it, guiding, protecting, directing as He sees fit.

Think about it.

Chapter 25 Appendix

Now there's a question worthy of any small group discussion: what does it mean to have dominion? Specifically, dominion ov er the planet? Over the animals? Over the family? To find answers, a good place to start would be with Adam. The groundwork was laid in Genesis 1:26 (NIV), *"God said, 'Lets us make mankind in our own image, in our likeness, so that they may rule over the fish in the sea and the birds in the sky, over the livestock and all the wild animals, and over all the creatures that move along the ground."* You want to talk about our mandate for ecological responsibility? It came a long time before Greenpeace and any other environmentalist you can name. And it was put into action from the very beginning, see also Genesis 2:19 (NIV), *"Now the Lord God had formed out of the ground all the wild animals and all the birds in the sky. He brought them to the man to see what he would name them; and whatever the man called each living creature, that was its name."*

And in case we need to be clear, look ahead to Genesis 9:3 where Noah and his family had survived the Great Flood. As they left the ark, they were told, "Everything that lives and moves about will be food for you. Just as I gave you the green plants, I now give you everything." Bottom line: it's okay to be a vegetarian, but don't do so for religious reasons.

Time moves on, and mankind learns more about "dominion". Animals are under our authority. Check. Children are under our authority Ephesians 6:1 (NIV), *"Children, obey your parents in the Lord, for this is right."*. Check. Wives are under the authority of husbands. Che... say what? That's the topic for another book, but it needs to be included in the whole idea of dominion. Everywhere we turn, God points us to this important truth: each and every one of us has a responsibility to wield authority and to be subject to those who hold authority over us. This includes how we treat animals, how we keep peace in the home, how we respond to our teachers, our parents, our bosses, and our God.

For Schnicklefritz and every other child on earth, learning and accepting the dominion mandate is a key to successful living. And helping those children understand is the responsibility given to everyone who lives in authority over them. Parents, siblings, extended family, teachers, pastors and anyone to whom God reaches out and says, "See that child? Be a role model."

Think about it.

Chapter 26 Appendix

1 Corinthians 2:9 (NIV) was one of my Dad's favourite verses, especially when the talk was about Heaven. His brother (my uncle) would go one and on about those streets of gold. His Dad (my Grandfather) would bring up the music, and how he was going to start an "angel choir". "Gotta help those folks understand the finer points of country western," he'd say. But then my Dad would bring the conversation to a close by quoting from Corinthians. "You're both wrong," he would insist. "Paul made it clear that, whatever Heaven was like, it was not what we imagined it to be." He'd laugh and say, "You know, I try to picture the best, most beautiful, most perfect place there could be, but then have to remind myself that it's not a picture of Heaven, because I just thought of it!"

We try to imagine what Schnicklefritz is going to be like. What traits is he going to pick up from his parents? How is his personality going to manifest itself, making him totally unique? At the end of the day, we have to accept the fact that such realities will just have to wait, and in the meantime, we may as well do something useful, like suck our thumbs.

Think about the things that still lie in your future. What experiences are you anticipating today? Keep in mind that "anticipation", by definition, means you're going to have to wait. Marsha and I have at least one marital incompatibility that's actually worked out for good. I like to enjoy things sooner rather than later, while Marsha prefers to savour good things as long as possible. Where this tendency plays out in the most obvious ways is during the Christmas season. I do have boundaries, mind you, but on the day after Thanksgiving, the tree goes up, the tinsel gets hung and Handel's Messiah starts playing all over the house. We all enjoy Christmas, then, since we're in Australia, Boxing Day, followed by New Years. Then on January 2nd, I'm ready to pack things up and move on. Marsha is still in "savour" mode, though, and won't let me take a single ornament down until at least February.

I talked about the "gift of growth" way back in chapter one, about how God, unencumbered by time, seems to go out of His way to see that we live under time's mandate. The water has to boil before we can make coffee, cheese has to ferment before it becomes cheddar, relationships have to develop before they become love (or something else entirely), and babies have to crawl before they can walk. And somewhere in all this, I believe, is that Divine lesson marked by "anticipation". No, I'm not going to give you the lesson; you'll have to work for it and then think about it.

Chapter 27 Appendix

If you have borne with me through these 27 letters, then I think you have a pretty good idea where I stand on the "pro-life" issue. In fact, if I didn't believe Schnicklefritz was a living being from the moment of his conception, then I wouldn't have spent so much time and energy talking to him for the past several months. I accept the fact that he was incapable of forming an intelligent reply from there in the womb, and even today we don't communicate much beyond the "ahhhhhh....boo!" level, which is quite satisfying to us both, by the way.

Then why all the fuss of compiling a stack of letters for whom the recipient has no appreciation? I have at least two answers for that. To begin with, Jeremiah has been given that "gift of growth" I talked about back in chapter one. He won't be a baby forever. There will come a day, God willing, when he will be ready and able to read this book, and in God's mercy, hopefully I'll be able to sit with him and talk about it together. My motivation in doing this is not so that he will say, "Wow, what a gifted author I have for a Grandpa!" No, I want him to look through these pages and see himself on every page. I want him to see the heritage into which he has been born. And above all, I want him to know with absolute assurance that he is loved, a condition that existed even before he made his appearance. Such an assurance is absolutely vital for successful living. Maybe that's why one of the best-known verses in the Bible, even among unbelievers, is John 3:16 (NIV). *"For so loved the world that whosoever believes in Him will not perish but have everlasting life."*

We don't have to look far to find examples of life without that assurance. To grow up believing that you are unloved, unwanted and unregarded is a certain formula for disaster, be it on a personal, a social or even a national level. I'll let history speak for itself.

Look with me at that other segment of society: those who regardless of their circumstance, can stand and say, "I am loved. I will not be diminished by the opinions of others, and I will not bow down to the gods of hate. There is no force, no philosophy, no creed that can dissuade me of that one Fact: I am loved, and that makes all the difference."

So why have I written and complied these letters? I want Jeremiah to know, to understand and to live by the knowledge that he has always been and always will be loved.

That was the first reason I wanted to share with you. The second is this: You are loved. I realize that there are many who cannot point to a loving mother and father. This saddens me almost beyond comprehension. I have known many over the years whose parents were either unknown or worse yet were cruel to their children. Many of those kids have overcome such tragic beginnings, and in most cases found the ability to do so because they came to know that their existence did not come about simply by human conception but by the Hand of a Creator God. The love that He has for His children cannot be compared to the love of us human mothers and fathers. It perseveres through all that life throws at us, and if we will allow it, will take us all the way to the place we call Heaven. There, we are told, *"He will wipe every tear from their eyes. There will be no more death or mourning or crying or pain, for the old order of things has passed away"* (Revelation 21:4 NIV).

Other Works by Tony and Marsha Woods

These and other books can be found by searching online (Amazon, etc) or by going directly to:
www.martonpublishing.com
For questions, please email: info@martonpublishing.com

Anagaion: *A Three-Part Discipleship Journey*

The Road Rising: *A One-Year Devotional Journey*

Leaving the Trail: *The Story of a Couple's Journey Toward the Kingdom (Sequel to "The Road Rising")*

Reaching the Heights: *The Trail Above (Third in the Triology)*

Looking for a Lamb: *A Father's Journey Up the Mountain of Grief and Beyond (Written following the death of Tony's Marsha's son, Trevor, to leukemia)*

On the Road With John: *A One-Year Devotional Study of the Fourth Gospel*

River Crossings: *Weekly Blogs From a Missionary in Thailand*

Sacrificed: *Given to an Empire, Found by God (Story of a former kamikaze pilot, led to faith by the Hand of God)*

Uncle Buddy: *Family Man for the Family of God*

Weaving Sunlight: *God's Tapestry of Two Lives (Memoirs* from the lives of Tony and Marsha)

Stop Me If You've Heard This (Every story ever told by Tony and Marsha)

www.ingramcontent.com/pod-product-compliance
Lightning Source LLC
Chambersburg PA
CBHW011342090426
42743CB00018B/3419